❋ 商务部十三五规划教材
❋ 跨境电子商务系列精品教材
❋ 全国外经贸职业教育教学指导委员会规划教材

跨境电商函电

Correspondence Writing in Cross-border E-commerce Transactions

主　编　陈祥国　孟雅楠

副主编　姚　元　苏晓娜　刘　畅　任　诤

编　者　袁秋红　窦　佳　郝冠军　梁燕丽

　　　　杜颖新　王　璐

中国商务出版社

图书在版编目（CIP）数据

跨境电商函电 = Correspondence Writing in Cross-border E-commerce Transactions / 陈祥国，孟雅楠主编 . —北京：中国商务出版社，2017. 6（2019.1重印）

商务部十三五规划教材　跨境电子商务系列精品教材

全国外经贸职业教育教学指导委员会规划教材

ISBN 978-7-5103-1929-7

Ⅰ. ①跨…　Ⅱ. ①陈… ②孟…　Ⅲ. ①电子商务-英语-电报信函-写作-职业教育-教材 Ⅳ. ①F713. 36

中国版本图书馆 CIP 数据核字（2017）第 165403 号

商务部十三五规划教材

跨境电子商务系列精品教材

全国外经贸职业教育教学指导委员会规划教材

跨境电商函电

Correspondence Writing in Cross-border E-commerce Transactions

陈祥国　　孟雅楠　主编

出　　　版：中国商务出版社

地　　　址：北京市东城区安定门外大街东后巷 28 号　　邮　编：100710

责任部门：职业教育事业部（010 – 64218072　295402859@ qq. com）

责任编辑：魏　红

总 发 行：中国商务出版社发行部 （010 – 64208388　64515150 ）

网　　　址：http：// www. cctpress. com

邮　　　箱：cctp@ cctpress. com

排　　　版：北京科事洁技术开发有限责任公司

印　　　刷：廊坊市长岭印务有限公司

开　　　本：787 毫米 ×1092 毫米　1/16

印　　　张：10. 25　　　　　　　字　　数：222 千字

版　　　次：2017 年 8 月第 1 版　　　印　　次：2019 年 1 月第 2 次印刷

书　　　号：ISBN 978-7-5103-1929-7

定　　　价：38. 00 元

Contents

Task 1　Laying out a Business E-mail

LEARNING OBJECTIVE:

☞ To learn how different parts of a business e-mail are arranged

Part 1　Getting to know your task

Scenario:

Aaron Li is the export manager of Qingdao Tianyi Arts and Crafts Import & Export Company. He'd like to meet his American client named James during his business trip in Los Angeles next month.

Task:

Write an e-mail on behalf of Aaron Li to James, asking whether you can meet in Los Angeles. The e-mail should be laid out in a proper form, based on the following information. The body of your e-mail has been given below. Divide it into paragraphs if necessary.

Aaron Li
Export Manager

Tianyi Arts & Crafts Imp. & Exp. Co., Ltd.
17/F Arts Bldg., 65 Taiping Rd., Qingdao 266071, P.R. China
Tel: 0086-532-82748906　　Fax: 0086-532-82748909
E-mail: aaron@tyarts.com.cn
Website: www.tyarts.com

James' e-mail account: james_bytn@ hotmail. com

The body of your e-mail is as follows:

I will go to LA on business 10th—13th next month, hoping we can meet then. Are you availa-

1

ble? Attached is a catalogue for our new products. Please check. If you are interested in some of them, please let me know so that I can take the samples to you. I am looking forward to your early reply.

Brainstorming：

What are the essential parts in the layout of an e-mail?

Part 2 | Learning about a similar task

在国际商务活动中，随着时代的发展和通信技术的进步，信息传递和交流的主要媒介也在不断变化和发展着。电子邮件、电话、传真、全球即时聊天工具如 Skype、WeChat 等已成为使用广泛的通讯方式。其中，电子邮件因其收发速度快、成本低廉且安全性较高而成为最流行的国际交流通信方式。

一、电子邮件的格式及书写规范

电子邮件的格式因网站的不同而不同，但其组成部分基本是一致的。例 1 和例 2 展示了商务电子邮件的邮件头和正文的基本要素。

例 1：外发的邮件

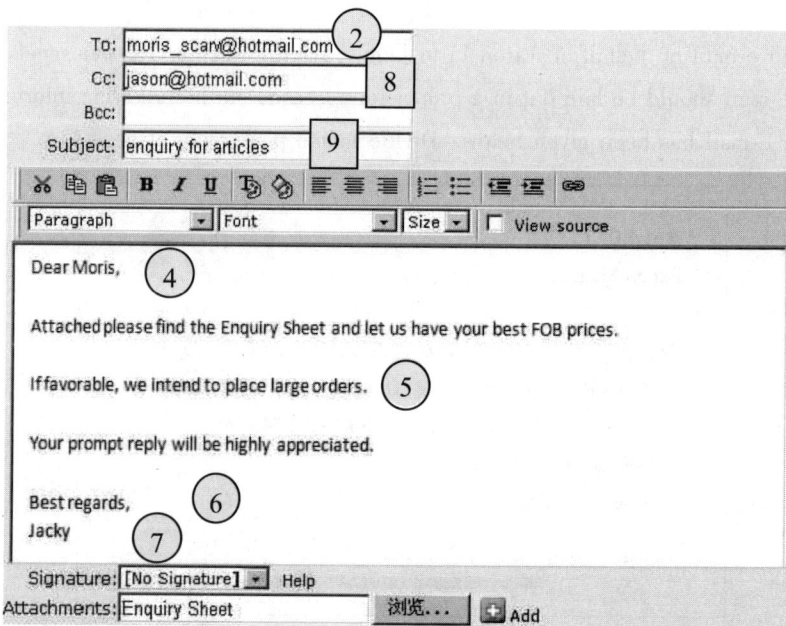

例2：收到的邮件

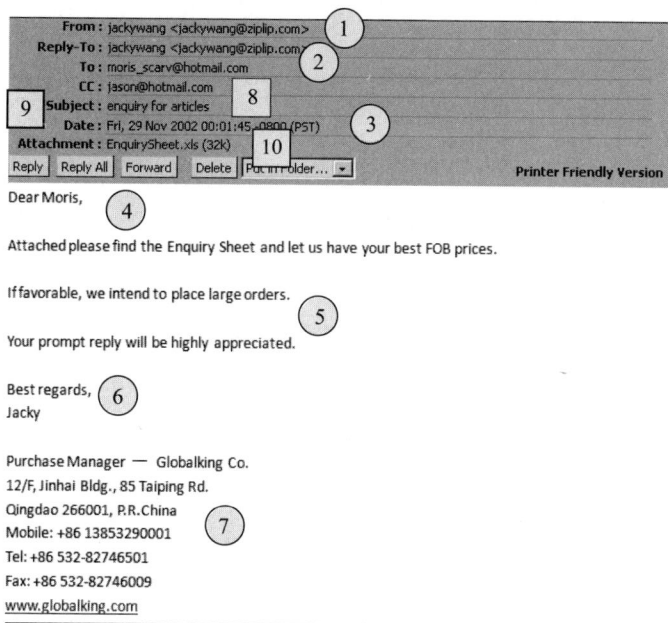

商务电子邮件包括7个基本组成部分和3个附加组成部分：

基本组成部分	①	发件人电子邮件地址	附加组成部分	⑧	抄送
	②	收件人电子邮件地址		⑨	事由
	③	日期		⑩	附件
	④	称呼			
	⑤	正文内容			
	⑥	结尾敬语			
	⑦	落款			

1. From：发件人电子邮件地址

发件人的电子邮件地址是由电子邮件服务器在收件人收到邮件时自动显示的，无须发件人手动键入。"Reply-To"后面就是发件人电子邮件地址，意思是直接回复给发件人。电子邮件的地址有统一的标准格式：用户名@服务器域名。@符号是电子邮件的定位符，通常读成"at"，也就是"在"的意思。在商务电子邮件中，用户名往往可以反映出发件人或收件人的姓名，而域名通常能反映出所使用的邮件服务商名称或者发件人/收件人的公司名称。

例3：电子邮件地址

taolimu@vip.126.com

3

jessica_tang@outlook.com

samuel.hill@sgs.com

221785932@qq.com

2. To：收件人电子邮件地址

此栏填写收件人的电子邮件地址。当收件人多于一人时，应该使用"；"号分隔电子邮箱地址，并按职务从高到低的顺序排列。

例4：群发电子邮件

To：mike.qiao@gmail.com；andley@hotmail.com；connie@hotmail.com

3. Date：日期

此栏由网站的服务器自动生成，不需要发件人手动键入，显示的是发件时间。英式日期格式是"日／月／年"的次序，而美式日期按"月／日／年"的次序。月份通常用英文单词（或缩写）来表示，避免用数字。日期用基数或序数表示。月份和日期之间不用逗号，月份和年份之间用不用逗号皆可，而日期和年份之前必须用逗号点开。此外，服务器通常还会显示"星期"、"钟点"等信息。有的邮件服务器显示日期用的是"Sent"，而不是"Date"。

例5：日期

Date：27th March，20-- 15:32	Date：16 April，20-- 08:25
Date：September 11st，20-- 4:56 PM	Date：Tuesday，February 26，20-- 11:25 AM

Sent：Fri.，July 12，20-- 9:20:23 GMT

4. Salutation：称呼

邮件的开头要称呼收件人。这既显得礼貌，也明确提醒该收件人此邮件是面向他（她）的，要求其给出必要的回应。使用何种称呼，要根据发件人的具体情况以及发件人与收件人之间的关系而定。此外，开头称呼应与结尾敬语相呼应。

称呼常用"Dear"开头，当不知道收件人姓名时，英式使用"Sir/Sirs"（男士）或"Madam/Mmes"（女士）来称呼，美式则使用"Gentlemen"或"Ladies/Gentlemen"，意思是"敬启者"；当知道收件人姓名时，正式场合一般使用 Mr.、Mrs.、Ms.、Miss 等尊称加收件人的家族姓；非正式场合或关系亲密时，可以直呼其名。但要注意：直呼对方的全名是非常不礼貌的。此外，称呼的首字母应使用英文大写。称呼后面一般使用"，"号，或不使用任何标点符号，"Gentlemen"后面使用"："号。

关系亲密的场合，有时还会用到"Hi"、"Hello"等非正式的用语。

4

例6：称呼

Dear Sir 或 Dear Madam 或 Dear Sir or Madam（Dear Sir/Madam），

Dear Sirs 或 Dear Sirs or Mmes，

Gentlemen：或 Ladies/Gentlemen：

To Whom It May Concern：

Dear Mr. Garnett，

Dear Stella，

Hi，Kevin 或 Hello，Kevin 或 Morning，Kevin

5. Body of E-mail：正文内容

正文内容是电子邮件最重要的部分，传递发件人的写信意图、详细信息和具体要求。正文格式一般采用齐头式（Blocked Style），即每行都是从最左侧开始写，不缩进，段落之间空一到两行。这种格式便于打字，节省时间，可提高工作效率。邮件正文语言表达要简练，尽量使用短小的句子和简短词语。

商务电子邮件的正文一般写有开头句和结尾句。开头句通常表达写信意图，或者确认收到某物并致以谢意。结尾句通常是表示友好和良好愿望的习惯用句。

例7：结尾句

Awaiting your good news.

Looking forward to your early reply.

We hope to receive your reply soon.

6. Complimentary Close：结尾敬语

结尾敬语是发件人在邮件结尾以礼貌的方式向收件人表达祝愿、勉慰之情的短语，意思是"××谨上"、"商祺"、"谨此致意"等。结尾敬语要根据发件人和收件人之间的关系选择用词，并与开头称呼相呼应。

在国际商务活动中，通常会与某一客户进行经常性邮件往来，因而"Best regards"和"Best wishes"成为国际商务邮件中最常用的结尾敬语。

结尾敬语中，只需要第一个单词的首字母大写，其余的单词全部小写。结尾敬语后可以加标点符号，也可以不加，应与开头称呼的标点符号保持一致。

开头称呼	结尾敬语	使用场合
Dear Sir(s) Dear Sir(s)/Madam(Mmes)	Yours faithfully Faithfully yours	正式场合 标准用法
Gentlemen Ladies/Gentlemen	Yours (very) truly Very truly yours	正式场合 美式表达
Dear Mr. Malone Dear Jenny	Yours sincerely/Sincerely Best wishes（英式） Best regards/Regards（美式）	非正式场合 双方熟悉场合

7. Signature：落款

电子邮件中的落款是邮件内容不可缺少的组成部分，既是对发件人信息（邮件显示信息）的补充，也是收件人进一步建立对发件人信任的必要信息。同时，电子邮件落款是一个公司品牌形象的组成部分，对企业网络品牌具有一定的影响。正规公司在邮件落款（尤其是对外部联系时的邮件）都有统一的格式设计，这样不仅看起来比较规范，而且也是体现了公司品牌形象。

落款包括发件人姓名、公司名称、地址、联系方式和网址等。

（1）发件人姓名可以是昵称、名或者全名。如："Belinda"、"Robert ZHANG"、"QIAO Yiya"。如今在国际商务信函中，中国商人更倾向于用汉语拼音大写来表示自己的姓，放在名前或名后，也方便了外国客户辨认。

（2）发件人如果有职务的话要写明，首字母大写。如："Sales Manager"。

（3）公司名称可以是全称或简称，还可以进一步写明部门。首字母应大写或全部字母大写。此外在签名栏显示公司标识和经营理念，也能起到很好的营销效果。

例8：发件人公司名称

- Shanghai Electric Import and Export Corporation
- AOL GL – Strategic Research & Innovation
- TAGLE SYSTEMS CORP.
- Salem Walmart Supercenter

（4）公司地址。在落款处标注发件人公司地址，有助于对方了解发件人公司的地理位置和通信方式。有些公司，在设计落款格式时则省略了公司地址信息。英语地址书写原则应遵循由小到大的顺序，先写门牌号码、街路名称，再写城市、省（州）和邮政区号，最后写国家名称。作为电子邮件结尾处的落款栏，公司地址应尽量设计在一行写完或分两行书写，不易分多行，否则签名栏过长，不美观。特别值得注意的是，地址中的标点符号需正确使用。习惯做法是：行末一般不加标点符号，但行中间该加标点的地方，还是不应省略；门牌号码与街道名称之间不加标点，但是在城市与国家名称之间必须用逗号分开。

例9：发件人公司地址

25 Farrindon Street，London，EC4A 4AB，U. K.

15/F，Highhope Mansion，91 Baixia Rd. Nanjing
210001，P. R. China

中国的地名可以用汉语拼音直译；一个地名只大写第一个字母，如"山东青岛"，可写作"Qingdao, Shandong"。地址中的常用简写，如：F.（=Floor，楼层）、Sec.（=Section，段）、Rd.（=Road，路）、Ave.（Avenue，街）、Blvd.（=boulevard，大道）、St.（=Street，街道）、Bldg.（=Building，楼）、Rm.（=Room，房间）、Ste.（=Suite，

套间)等。

（5）发件人联系方式。通常包括手机(Mobile，或简写为 M)、固定电话(简写为 Tel 或 PH)、传真(Fax)的号码、电子邮件地址以及国际实时通讯工具账号、如 Skype 账号等。其中，国际电话由国家电话区号 + 当地城市电话区号 + 当地电话号码组成。

例 10：发件人联系方式

> Mobile：+86 138 - 2035 - 7117
>
> Tel：+86 - 10 - 5969 - 3208
>
> Fax：+86 - 10 - 5969 - 3202
>
> Skype：martin. tang@ hotmail. com

（6）发件人公司网址。能够方便客户通过浏览网站，了解更多发件人公司和产品的信息，起到宣传和营销的作用。

例 11：落款

> Yours faithfully，
>
> TobyWalsh
> Program Director
>
> AOL GL - Strategic Research & Innovation
> Mobile：+4791659227
> toby. walsh@ aolgl. com

> Best regards，
> Selina Zhong
> Sales Manager
> JIELI PLASTIC
> LEADING INJECTION PLASTICS MANUFACTURER
>
> QINGDAO JIELI INDUSTRIAL CO. LTD
> NO. 398，EAST YUTAI STREET，QINGDAO CITY，260012，CHINA
> PH：(86) 532 - 86578701 FAX：(86) 532 - 86578702
> EMAIL：selina@ jlplastics. com
> M：0086 - 15263753016
> WWW. JLPLASTICS. COM

8. Cc 和 Bcc：明抄和暗抄

抄送分为明抄和暗抄。

"Cc"(Carbon copy)明抄：如果发件人想让收件人知道该邮件同时发给了第三方即被抄送人，可在 Cc 后填加被抄送人的电子邮件地址，这叫做明抄送。明抄送的目的是告知，被明抄送的人不需回应，当然如果被明抄送的人有建议，也可回复邮件。

例 12：明抄

> To：sales. dept@ gmail. com
> Cc：purchase. dept@ gmail. com

收件人是销售部，同时邮件明抄送给采购部；销售部知道采购部也收到了这封邮件。

"Bcc"（Blind carbon copy）暗抄：如果发件人不想让收件人知道这封信抄送给了谁，则在 Bcc 处填写被抄送人的电子邮件地址即可，这叫做暗抄送，也叫密送。

例 13：暗抄

> To：zac_ efron@ walmart. com. us
> Bcc：lukas. thibaut@ walmart. com. us

收件人是 Mr. ZacEfron，同时邮件暗抄送给 Mr. LukasThibaut；Mr. ZacEfron 不知道 Mr. Lukas Thibaut 也收到这封邮件。

9. Subject：主题

主题是邮件的事由或标题。主题应该明确，用少量的关键词说明邮件要阐明的问题，以引起收件人重视，尽快处理，并方便以后查找。主题中句首的单词和专有名词的首字母应该大写，或者也可将除了少于 5 个字母的介词、连接词或冠词之外的每一个单词的首字母大写。

当收件人回复（reply）或全部回复（reply to all）邮件时，主题栏会自动在原主题词句前显示"Re："字样，表示"关于"该主题；当收件人转发（forward）邮件时，主题栏会自动在原主题词句前显示"Fw："字样，表示"转发"该主题。当然，发件人也可以不使用这样自动产生的主题词句，而自行设定邮件主题。

例 14：主题

> Subject：Item No. 125 packaging

> Subject：Please Amend L/C No. 281 ASAP. Important！！！

> Subject：Re：Item No. 125 packaging

> Subject：Fw：Please Amend L/C No. 281ASAP. Important！！！

10. Attachment：附件

也可用"Attached"表示，即在附件中添加文件、图片等。如果邮件带有附件，应在正文里面提示收件人查看附件。邮件的附件必须写上题目，能够概括附件的内容，方便收件人下载后管理。附件数目较多时应打包压缩成一个文件。此外，邮件服务器会清楚显示出所附文件或图片的格式及大小。带有附件的邮件，通常会被系统标注一个曲别针记号"〗"，提醒收件人此邮件有附件。

例15：附件

Attachment：Packing List. xls（0. 46K）

Attachment：Brochure for Wigs. pdf（4. 7M）

Attachment：Pictures for samples#103～114. zip（5. 6M）

二、商务电子邮件的写作原则

商务电子邮件的写作应遵循清楚（Clarity）、简洁（Conciseness）和礼貌（Courtesy）的原则，即3C原则。

1. 清楚（Clarity）

清楚原则指层次清楚，用词准确。内容要适当分段并尽量使用短段落，必要时可标上段落号；用词要准确，切忌使用语义模糊、模棱两可的词或词组，以免产生歧义，造成误解，延误商务沟通和贸易。

2. 简洁（Conciseness）

简洁原则是商务英语写作最重要的原则，指在不影响完整性和礼貌性的前提下，尽量使用简单句子和简短词语（如缩略语），这样不仅能节约双方的时间，让人一目了然，而且还能给对方以干练和高效的良好印象。一封拖沓冗长、措辞复杂的电子邮件既浪费时间，也会给阅读者带来不必要的麻烦。

3. 礼貌（Courtesy）

礼貌原则指措辞婉转，语气自然诚恳，礼貌得体，使对方容易接受，同时遵守国际商务往来惯例，尊重对方风俗习惯。注意做到：（1）表示批评、建议、要求时，避免使用命令和生硬的口气，多用友好、肯定的语气和适当使用被动语态；（2）适当使用虚拟语气、委婉语气等提出要求；（3）对坏消息表示歉意，并说明问题的原因；（4）回复邮件要及时。

除了以上原则外，商务电子邮件的写作还应该遵循准确（Correctness）、完整（Completeness）、体谅（Consideration）和具体（Concreteness）的原则。

三、跨境电商平台站内信的格式

跨境电子商务中与客户的交流方式除了电子邮件之外，还有电子商务平台站内信这种普遍使用的方式。常用的电子商务平台如亚马逊（Amazon）、速卖通（AliExpress）、敦煌网（Dhgate）等站内信的组成部分基本是一致的。例16展示了站内信形式，例17展示了站内消息记录。

例 16：站内信

在例 16 中，①是收信人，②是书写正文的地方，③是上传附件，④是回到消息记录。相对于正规的商务邮件格式而言，站内信正文的书写则较为简单，一般包括称呼、正文、结尾敬语、落款这四部分。格式和书写规范与电子邮件的要求一样。在实际业务中，有时会不拘泥于固定格式，省略掉称呼、结尾敬语和签名，直接写正文内容。

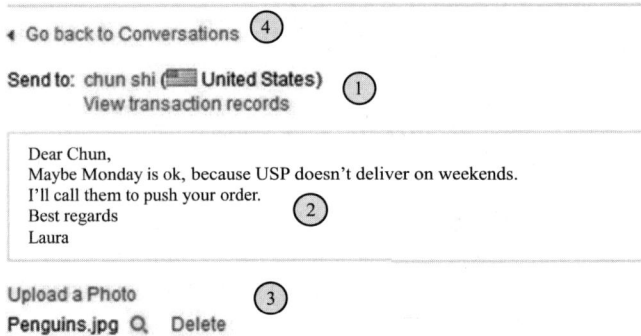

客户收到站内信后，有时会通过站内信进行回复。这样买方双方可以通过站内信多次交流沟通，如例 17。

例 17：站内消息记录

Part 3 **Getting prepared for your task**

Ⅰ. Put the following addresses into right order and translate the Chinese addresses into English.

1. GreatRussellStreet, London, No. 66, CamdenTown, UK, WC1B 3DG

2. 10036, 520, New York, USA, 12th Avenue

3. 青岛市市南区香港中路 59 号国际金融中心 1205 室 邮编：266072

4. 中国北京市东长安街 2 号 邮编：100731

Ⅱ. Correct the mistakes about the layout, parts and expressions in the following e-mail and start a new paragraph where necessary.

To:	horris@dqs.com
Cc:	
Subject:	
Attachment:	

Dear Manager:

Thanks for your offer for "Compaq" Brand Key Boards. We feel regretful that our buyers find your price a little high. If a 10% reduction can be reached, we can assure you that substantial business will materialize. Looking forward to your kind comments.

Best regard

cliff, purchasing manager

Beijing ITF Hardware Products Imp. & Exp. Corp.

28 Dong An Men Street

86-010-62536891

Ⅲ. Fill in each blank in a proper form according to the following information.

Recipient's name：Gilbert

Recipient's e-mail account：hintingwro@ gmail. com

cc：qilida@ kh. com. cn

The body of the e-mail：

Your e-mail of Mar. 16 has been noted with thanks. We agree to change the quantities considering our long term friendly relationship. Attached is the new P/I made out accordingly in PDF. Please sign back if everything is OK.

Sender's name：Helen Fang, Sales Manager of Kanghai International Trading Co., Ltd.

Sender's address：10/F Fuda Bldg., 132 Gutian Rd.,

Fuzhou 350001, P. R. China

Sender's contact information：   Tel：0591 − 28564625

Fax：0591 − 28564672

E-mail：helen. fang@ kh. com. cn

Sender's company website：www. kanghai. com

To:	
Cc:	
Subject:	

Part 4   Getting your task done

Now please write an e-mail based on your task in Part 1.

To:	
Cc:	
Subject:	

Task 2   Launching a New Product

LEARNING OBJECTIVE:

☞ To be able to launch[1] new products on an e-business platform

Part 1   Getting to know your task

Scenario:

This artificial flower Item No. BRI26438 shown in the following picture is your latest product. You are releasing a new product on your trade platform[2]. In order to attract your customers and receive more attention, you should demonstrate the strengths of your products and your company in a brief and appealing way.

Task:

Describe briefly all the information related to your product, your company and your service, and complete the tables below:

Brainstorming:

What information should you provide about a new product when you are launching it in the market?

NOTES：

1. launch：*vt.* 发布/推出（产品）

The company announced it will launch a new version of its software in January.

这家公司宣布一月份将发布软件的新版本。

也可以用 to release a product。

2. trade platform：*n.* 交易平台

产品简介：

产品类型：人造花	材料：塑料	产地：青岛，中国（大陆）
品牌：Bright	货号：BRI26438	长度：32″/102cm
特点：高仿真	ODM/OEM：接受	
用途：花园、家居、酒店、公园、办公室、学校装饰		
颜色：见图片		使用寿命：用作室内装饰 5~8 年

公司简介：

Qingdao Bright Artificial Plants Co., Ltd 成立于20--年（已核实），位于山东省（已核实），拥有员工 100 名，是一家具有多年出口经验的假花制造商。占地面积 5000 平方米，月生产能力 20 万件，拥有研发部、销售部、生产部和质检部。主要产品包括人造椰子树、人造棕榈树、人造樱桃和桃子、人造生态墙，人造植物等，年出口额 50 万美元。产品主要销往：国内市场，占 21%；南美市场 16%；北美市场 15%

业务简介：

接受个性化定制商标
接受第三方验货
著名设计师设计，工厂直接销售认证

残次品处理：

所有残次品或质量问题（除了在运输中造成的）均在下批货中补偿
因残次品或者质量问题所造成的客户的损失将在下批货中得到补偿

信用保证：

使用一达通

交付周期：

ODM 订单为 1~5 个工作日，生产周期 7~45 天；OEM 订单为 7~15 个工作日，生产周期 7~45 天，接受加急订单

质检：

所有产品在生产过程中均经过 5 道检验；
原材料在生产前进行检验；
每道工序结束后进行全面检验；
装运前进行全面检验

样品费用：

样品生产前全款付样品费

Part 2 Learning about a similar task

WNE Co., Ltd. Profile

A released product
Artificial Silk Flower

WNE Co. Ltd (Guangzhou) is one of the branches of WNE Company, which was founded in 20--. A small shop selling artificial plants and wedding decoration products 16 years ago has been developed into a big manufacturer in China, running more than 10 branches in Guangzhou and Shenzhen now.

Product details：

Plant type：Flowers	Material[1]：Silk flower plastic stems	Place of origin[2]：Guangzhou, China (Mainland)
Brand：WNE	Item No.：CL－MA80	Length：50cm
Character：superior quality and realistic looking[3]	ODM[4]/OEM[5]：warmly accepted	
Use：wedding, home, hotel, festival, restaurant for indoor decoration		
Color：white/pink/purple	Life time[6]：>5 years (indoor)	

NOTES：

1. material：n. 原材料

raw material 原料

finished product 成品

semi-finished product 半成品

2. place of origin：n. 产地

3. realistic looking：外观逼真

4. ODM：Original Design Manufacturer 原始设计制造商

5. OEM：Original Equipment Manufacturer 原始设备制造商

6. life time：使用寿命

Company profile[1]：

Business Type[2]：manufacturer	Location：Guangzhou, China (verified[3])
Total annual revenue[4]：USD 300 Million	Year established：20—— (verified)
Main Products：artificial trees, artificial cherry trees, artificial flower walls, artificial wedding centerpieces	
Top 3 markets：Western Europe 70%, North America 10%, Middle East 8%	
Floor area[5]：2,000 square meters	Monthly Capacity[6]：1 million pieces
Departments：Production Dept[7]. Sales Dept. Purchase Dept[8]. QC Dept[9].	

NOTES:

1. profile: n. 简介
2. business type: 业务类型
3. verified: 已核实
4. total annual revenue: 总年收入
5. floor area: 占地面积
6. monthly capacity: 月生产能力
7. Production Department: 生产部
8. Purchase Department: 采购部
9. QC Dept.: Quality Control Department 质检部

Brainstorming:

What else can we mention when we release our new products? Please tick the appropriate box(es).

☐ Your service
☐ Your guarantee
☐ Credit guarantee
☐ Quality control

Other advantages:

Payment terms:	Visa Credit Card[1], MasterCard Credit Card[2], T/T[3] for online orders L/C[4], T/T, Western Union[5] Payment for offline orders
Our service:	1. Unique design by famous designers 2. Customized[6] logos 3. Third party[7] inspection accepted
Our guarantee:	1. Customers' interests fully guaranteed[8] 2. Defective products[9] (besides those damage during transportation) can be replaced in the next order 3. Losses caused by quality problems are compensated[10] for in the next order
Credit guarantee[11]:	Trade Assurance[12] Escrow Service[13]
Lead time[14]:	For ODM items: 1~5 working days; for OEM items: 7~15 working days
Quality Control[15]:	All products must go through five checks in manufacturing process[16] Relevant material check before production Full check after every process Full check before shipping
Sample fees[17]:	Sample fees should be fully paid before making the sample.

NOTES：

1. Visa Credit Card：VISA 信用卡

2. MasterCard Credit Card：万事达信用卡

3. T/T：电汇 全称 Telegraphic Transfer 用法详解见 Task 9

4. L/C：全称 Letter of Credit 信用证　用法详解见 Task 9

5. Western Union：西联汇款

6. customize：*v.* 定制

We can customize your clocks with your logo，size，name and images.

我们根据您的标识、尺寸，名字和图片来定制钟表。

7. third party：第三方

8. guarantee：*v.* 保证

9. defective product：不合格产品

10. compensate：*v.* 补偿，赔偿

compensate sb. for sth. 赔偿，补偿某人……

We have to claim against you to compensate us for the loss，i. e. USD3,178.

我方不得不向你方提出 3178 美元的损失赔偿。

We regret the losses you have suffered and agree to compensate you by USD1,000.

我方对你方遭受的损失深表歉意，同意向你方赔偿 1000 美元。

compensation：*n.* 补偿，赔偿

make compensation for sb. 's loss 补偿某人的损失

We trust you will agree that we cannot be expected to make compensation for your dam aged toys.

我方相信你方同意我们不赔偿损坏的玩具。

11. credit guarantee：信用保证

12. Trade Assurance：a free service by Alibaba. com that's designed to help create trust between buyers and suppliers. Trade Assurance helps buyers in the event of shipping and quality-related dispute. 一达通，阿里巴巴信用保障服务

13. Escrow Service：又称为国际支付宝，是阿里巴巴专门针对国际贸易推出的一种第三方支付担保交易服务，英文全称 Alibaba. com's Escrow Service

14. lead time：交货期

15. quality control：质量检验

16. process：*n.* 工序

17. sample fee：样品费用

Useful expressions

Strengths of your plants and goods 工厂及产品优势

We are a leading garment accessory and jewelry supplier with 8 years' experiences in exporting.
我们是一家大型的服装配件和珠宝供货商，拥有 8 年出口经验。
Our first priority is to provide goods of superior quality and premium service.
我们的第一要务是为客户提供质量上乘的产品和最优质的服务。
We have more than 200 kinds of products of various color selections and more than 800 raw materials in stock.
工厂库存 200 多种不同样式和颜色的产品，800 多种原材料。
Please note that our delivery date mainly depends on specification of the goods and the quality.
请注意我们的交货期取决于具体产品类型和产品数量。
We can assure you that our goods are of superior quality, all of which can reach European Import Standard.
我们只销售高质量的产品，所有产品均达到欧洲进口标准。
We are willing to make the goods as per your customized size, OEM and ODM orders are warmly accepted.
我们接受 OEM 和 ODM 订单，可以按照您定制的尺寸进行生产。
Our plant covers floor area of 4,500 square meters with Production Department, Sales Department, Quality Control Department and Purchase Department. The monthly capacity is 200,000 pieces with total annual revenue USD3,000,000.
我们工厂占地面积 4500 平方米，月生产能力 20 万件，年收入 300 万美元，设有生产部、销售部、质检部和采购部。
There are multiple colors to select, please refer to the pictures for detailed information.
我们的产品有多种颜色可供选择，具体颜色请参考图片。
Our goods have been strictly checked before shipment, we can assure you that the defective goods can be replaced or the losses can be refunded in the next order.
我们有严格的质检程序，如果货物中有残次品，我们保证在下批货中补寄或者尽快退款。
All the inquiries for our goods will be replied within 24 hours.
所有关于产品的询盘在 24 小时内答复。

Positive feedbacks 获得好评

We have won many positive feedbacks at AliExpress.
我们在速卖通的好评很多。
We've been doing business on eBay for many years and are quite confident about our products.
我们一直在 eBay 做业务，对于我们的产品很有信心。
Our store has been awarded 3 diamonds, which means we have received more than 2,000 feedbacks from our customers around the world.
我们的店信誉已达到了三钻，这意味着我们已经收到了来自全球两千多名顾客的评价反馈。
More than 800 customers have added our store to their My Favorites tab.
已有 800 多名顾客把本店添加到收藏夹里。

Part 3 Getting prepared for your task

I. Pattern drills. Make sentences with the following italicized expressions.

1. *We are a* leading garment accessory and jewelry supplier with 8 years' experiences in exporting.

A. 我们是一家经营化工类产品出口的私营企业。

B. 我们是一家综合性的集团，业务主要涉及家电出口和房地产。

C. 我们是宜家(IKEA)的供货商，主要经营家具产品出口已经 15 年了。

D. 我们是一家中美合资企业，经营纺织产品出口。

2. *I can assure you that* you will find very good prospects in our products.

A. 我可以向你保证我们的商品很有竞争力。

B. 我们可以保证这个产品的将有良好的销售市场。

C. 我们可以保证我们的月生产能力能够达到10000 件。

D. 我们可以保证在保修期内免费退货。

3. *We* have more than 200 *kinds of products of various color selections* and more than 800 raw materials in stock.

A. 你可以有多种多样的选择。

B. 这类发带有多种型号供您选择。

C. 我们公司有各种价格水平的产品供您选择。

D. 园艺工具有各种型号供您选择。

II. Translate the following categories into Chinese and match the following commodities with the right categories.

Category	Commodity
Machinery, Industrial parts & Tools ( )	E-cigarette
Health and Beauty ( )	Women's Cashmere Crew Neck Sweater
Sports and Toys ( )	Elegant Crown Paper Cutting
Apparel, Textiles & Accessories ( )	LLDPE Stretch Film for Packaging
Packaging, Advertising & Office ( )	Premium Stainless steel Mini Garden Shovel
Metallurgy, Chemicals & Rubber ( )	Jade Bracelet for Women
Home, Lights & Construction ( )	German Technology Solid Rubber Tyres for Cars 205/60
Electrical Equipment, components & Telecom ( )	LED High Brightness Light
Jewelry, Bags and Shoes ( )	Hot-selling Outdoor Sports Equipment Step-teller Bracelet(计步手环)

Ⅲ. Express briefly your advantages in phrases.

价格优惠，质量上乘	_____
最新设计，工艺精湛	_____
规格颜色可选择性多	_____
接受定制，物流迅速	_____
接受 OEM 和 ODM	_____
专业物流和质检	_____
货源稳定，交货期短	_____
低起订量，交货迅速	_____

Ⅳ. Translate the following e-shop introduction into Chinese.

An introduction to an e-shop

Dear customers,

Welcome to visit our E-shop http://www. ebay. XXX.

Guangzhou Brilliant Wig Co. , Ltd. has been in the line of producing wigs for 18 years and can produce more than 3 ,000 kinds of wigs with two product lines: synthetic fiber products and human hair products. Our products, which are of superior quality, competitive price and timely delivery have been exported to 36 countries so far.

Our online shop specializes in the sales of our products, demonstrating all of our products and general information. If you need more information, just leave us your message. The latest pictures of the products and relative information will be updated within 24 hours.

We also welcome your ODM orders and OEM orders. If you have any questions, please contact our customer service.

Best wishes,

Eric

Part 4　Getting your task done

Please complete the three tables in Part 1 based on the information given below and release your product online concisely:

Product details:

Plant type:		Material:		Place of origin:
Brand:		Item Number:		Length:
Character:			ODM/OEM:	
Use:				
Color:			Life time:	

Company profile：

Business Type：	Location：
Total annual revenue：	Year established：
Main Products：	
Top 3 markets：	
Floor area：	Monthly Capacity：
Departments：	

Other advantages：

Our service：	
Our guarantee：	
Credit guarantee：	
Lead time：	
Quality control：	
Sample fee：	

Task 3　Establishing Trade Relations

LEARNING OBJECTIVE:

☞ To be able to write an e-mail to establish trade relations with a new client

Part 1　Getting to know your task

Scenario:

Alex Zhao, Sales Director[1] in Qingdao Bright Artificial Plants Co., Ltd, gets a business card from TJMAX HOMEWARE at China Imp. & Exp. Fair[2], where Mr. Bach, Chairman of TJMAX HOMEWARE shows his interest in Artificial Flower Item No[3]. BRI26438. The unit price for Item No. BRI26438 is USD1. 2/piece FOB Qingdao.

Additionally, Qingdao Bright Artificial Plants Co. , Ltd is capable of making products as per customized sizes. Their key customers include Cask, Weeland and Ailpress.

Qingdao Bright Artificial Plants Co., Ltd.

Add: No. 26 Zhanshan Road, Qingdao, 266019, China

Tel: +86 − 532 − 85621017

Mobile: +86 − 18662168989

Website: www. brightplant. com

Task:

Write an e-mail to ask for establishment of trade relations with the company indicated in the card below.

Robert Bach
Chairman & CEO

TJMAX HOMEWARE

715 Market Street
Wilmington, North Carolina,
28425, USA　　　　**TJMAX**
TEL: 1-910-508-8030　**HOMEWARE**
Email: robertbach@tjmax.com

Brainstorming：

If you write a first letter or E-mail to someone you want to sell your products to,

what information would you like them to know?

NOTES：

1. Sales Director：销售经理，销售总监
2. China Imp. & Exp. Fair：简称 Canton Fair 广交会
3. Item No.：表示编号的商品、列表中的商品

还可以用：Article No.（Art. No.）

This list comprises the main items the exporter deals in.

此清单包括该出口商经营的主要商品。

Part 2 Learning about a similar task

Sample e-mail 1：Sellers asking to establish trade relations(1)

From：Tonyzhang@ cherry. com
To：berrysmith@ terseed. com
Subject：Cherry Shell Carving/15% special offer for the first container
Attachment：Price list. pdf(1. 5M)
Dear Mr. Smith,   We are very glad to know you from your website and note you are the largest wholesaler[1] of shell carvings[2] with an excellent reputation in Poland and would like to find a reliable supplier in China.   We are Cherry Shell Carvings Imp. & Exp. Co., Ltd., mainly dealing in[3] the export of Shell Carvings for 20 years and would like to establish trade relations with you at an early date.   Our online shop http://www. alibaba. com. XXX demonstrates all the products with photos and specifications, which will give you detailed information about the items you interest.   In order to push the sales of[4] our products at your end, we are willing to grant you a 15% discount as a special offer for the first container.   Attached please find[5] our latest price list. If you find something interesting, we will send our

samples via air[6] on receipt of[7] your specific inquiry[8].

We look forward to[9] your favorable reply.

Best regards,
Tony Zhang
Sales Manager for Cherry Shell Carving Imp. & Exp. Co. , Ltd.
Add：65 Xianggang Dong Rd. , Qingdao, China
Mobile：+86 - 18653287654
Tel：+86 - 532 - 66712016
Fax：+86 - 532 - 66712016
Website：www. cherryarts. com

NOTES：

1. wholesaler：批发商

2. shell carving：*n.* 贝雕品

3. deal in：经营

Our company deals in home textiles for over 15 years.

我们公司经营家具纺织品 15 年。

还可以用 handle、trade in、be engaged in 以及 specialize in(专营)等。

We have been handling the export of nuts for many years and would like to establish trade relations with you at an early date.

我们经营干果出口已有多年，希望与贵方建立业务联系。

Specializing in export of printed tablecloth, we wish to express our desire to establish trade relations with you.

我们专营印花桌布出口，希望贵方建立业务联系。

4. push the sales of ：促销

还可以说：promote the products。

We sincerely appreciate the effort you have made for pushing the sales of our products.

我们真诚地感激贵方在促销我方产品方面所做出的努力。

5. Attached please find. . . ：随附……，请查收

Attached please find our quotation sheet for our latest products available for export.

随附最新可供出口产品报价单，请查收。

6. via air：通过空邮

7. on/upon receipt of：一收到……就(立即)……

We will make duplicate samples on receipt of your sample fees.

一收到贵方样品费，我方立即制作复样。

8. specific inquiry：具体询盘

9. look forward to：期待

We are looking forward to meeting you again.

期待与您再次见面。

We look forward to your favorable reply.

盼佳音。

Sample e-mail 2：Sellers asking to establish trade relations(2)

From：peterson@ sunshine. com
To：jacobwoods@ terseed. com
Subject：Sunshine Decorating Products/IKEA supplier
Attachment：Price list. pdf(1. 5M)

Dear Jacob,

I am Peterson, the sales manager of Sunshine Decorating Products Imp. & Exp. Co., Ltd., a leading home decorating products manufacturer in China. We had a pleasant talk last week at the Canton Fair, from which I knew that you were interested in wood card makings. Please take your time to know our company as follows[1]：
——Capacity：30,000 m^2 workshops, 40—60 HQ[2]/month
——Key customers：IKEA[3]
——Factory Audit：BSCI[4]
Also, we would like to offer[5] you some of our best sellers[6] as follows：
Wood rabbit for card making@ USD1. 25/PC FOB Qingdao[7]
Wood bird for card making@ USD1. 10/PC FOB Qingdao

Welcome to visit our E-shop：http://www. ebay. XXX, from which you could know more about our products.

Attached please find our latest illustrated price list[8]. Please let me know other items you are interested in so as to enable me to send the samples to you ASAP[9].

We look forward to your favorable reply.

Best regards,
Tony Zhang
Sales Manager for Sunshine Imp. & Exp. Co., Ltd.
Add：65 Xianggang Dong Rd., Qingdao, China
Mobile：+86 –18653287654

Tel：+86 - 532 - 66712016
Fax：+86 - 532 - 66712016
Website：www. cherryarts. com

NOTES：

1. as follows：如下，以下

The specifications of the goods now available for export are as follows.

可供出口的货物规格如下。

类似表达方式：

the following *n.* 下面内容

I will explain further with the following.

我会用以下内容进一步说明。

the following *adj.* 下面的

The following items were the best sellers last year.

以下产品是去年的畅销品。

2. HQ：High Cubic 的简称，即 40 尺集装箱高柜

3. IKEA：宜家公司

4. BSCI：商业社会标准认证

5. offer：*v.* 报盘，用法详解见 Task 4

6. best seller：畅销品

7. @ USD 1. 25/PC FOB Qingdao：单价每件 1. 25 美元，青岛装运港船上交货价

8. illustrated price list：带图解价格单

illustrated catalogue：带图解目录

9. ASAP：尽快，as soon as possible 缩写形式

Useful expressions

Source of information 消息来源
We got your name from www. alibaba. com and noted that you are interested in arts and crafts. 我们从阿里巴巴网得知贵公司正在求购工艺品。 We had your name and address from the advertising on the newspaper and knew that you are a leading wholesaler of textiles in your country. 我们从报纸广告上得知贵公司是贵国最大纺织品批发商。 We had a brief talk at the Canton Fair held in April this year, where you showed your interest in our products. 我们在 4 月举行的广交会进行了简短交谈，贵方对我方产品表示出了浓厚的兴趣。

Your company was kindly introduced/recommended to us by our raw material supplier in China, as a prospective buyer of canned foodstuffs.

我们在中国供货商将贵公司介绍/推荐给了我方，说你们是罐装食品的潜在买主。

Business scope 经营范围
We mainly deal in the import and export of textiles for many years, and would like to establish trade relations with you at an early date. 我们主要经营纺织品进出口已有多年，希望早日与贵方建立业务联系。 We have been handling the export of teapots for more than 15 years. 我们经营茶壶出口已有 15 年以上了。 We have been in the line of peanuts processing for 10 years and are willing to enter into business relations with you. 我们经营花生加工有 10 年了，想与贵方建立业务联系。 Specializing in the export of light industrial products, we would like to establish trade relations with you. 我方专营轻工业产品出口，想与贵方建立业务联系。

Attachment 附件
Out latest price list is attached. 随函附我方最新价格单。 Attached are the pictures of our samples taken from four sides. 随函附从四个角度拍摄的样品照片。 Attached please find our Purchase Order in PDF file. 随函附 PDF 格式订单，请查收。

Part 3　Getting prepared for your task ▷ ▷▷ ▷▷

Ⅰ. Pattern drills. Make sentences with the following italicized expressions.

1. *We are very glad to know you from* your website and note that you are the largest wholesaler of Shell Carvings with an excellent reputation in Poland and would like to find a reliable supplier in China.

A. 我们很高兴地从阿里巴巴网上得知贵公司是一家著名的假花进口商正在中国寻求合作伙伴。

B. 我们很高兴地从广告中得知贵公司正在求购纯棉印花桌布(cotton printed table cloth)

C. 我们从 4 月北京举办的国际天然保健品展销会(International Exhibition of Natural Health Products)得知贵公司是一家声誉良好的保健品进口企业，希望从中国进口一批保健品。

D. 我们很高兴地从商会(Chamber of Commerce)得知贵公司是美国最大的枸杞(goji

berries)零售商，希望能与您建立业务联系。

2. We are Cherry Shell Carvings Imp. & Exp. Co., Ltd., mainly *dealing in* the export of Shell Carvings for 20 years.

A. 我们从 20-- 年开始经营纺织品出口业务。

B. 我们主要经营配件(accessories)类产品的加工出口，产品主要包括：厕所配件 (bathroom accessories)及厨房配件(kitchen accessories)。

C. 我们经营罐装食品出口已有 25 年的历史。

D. 我们是一家中美合资企业，主要经营塑料产品出口。

3. *Attached please find* our latest price list.

A. 随函附最新价格单，请查收。

B. 随函附产品照片，请查收。

C. 随函附产品说明，请查收。

D. 随函附报价单，请查收。

Ⅱ. Supply the missing words in the blanks with the words given.

one	reply	on	by	introduce
enter	relations	specific	in	as

Dear Sir or Madam,

Learning from the Commercial Counselor's office of our Embassy(使馆商务参赞处) _____ your country that you are _____ of the leading importers of canned foodstuffs, we have the pleasure of _____ ourselves to you _____ a state corporation specializing in the export of canned foodstuffs, and express our desire to _____ into business _____ with you.
In order to give you a general idea of our canned goods, we attach our latest catalogue. Quotations and samples will be sent _____ air _____ receipt of your _____ inquiry.
We look forward to your favorable _____.
Best wishes,
Katy

Ⅲ. Choose the best answer to complete each of the following sentences.

1. We are looking forward to _____ from you soon.
    A. hearing　　B. hear　　C. heard　　D. be heard
2. Your name and address _____ to us by Chamber of Commerce of London.
    A. have given　　B. have been given　　C. give　　D. given
3. As the goods _____ within the scope of our business activities, please contact us at once.
    A. falls　　B. fall　　C. falling　　D. fell
4. We shall send you four samples _____ receipt of your inquiries.

     A. in   B. at   C. for   D. upon

5. We hope to enter _____ business relations _____ your firm.

     A. into, with   B. with, into   C. /, at   D. with, at

Ⅳ. Translate the following e-mail into English.

Jackline，你好，

我是青岛玲玲手工艺品进出口有限公司销售经理 Nicky Wang。我们从阿里巴巴网上得知贵公司每年从中国进口陶瓷(porcelain)和玉雕(jade carving)。我们经营这种产品已有多年，想借此机会与你建立业务联系。

中国的手工艺品(handicrafts)以品质精良，工艺精湛，式样新颖而闻名于世。为了使你们对我们的产品有所了解，随函附最新带图解目录供你方参考。

盼佳音。

青岛玲玲手工艺品进出口有限公司

Nicky Wang

Sales Manager

Qingdao Lingling Handicrafts Imp. & Exp. Co., Ltd.

Add：No. 868 Haier Rd., Laoshan District, Qingdao, 266001, China

Tel：+86 - 18661706666

E-mail：nickywang@163. com

Part 4　Getting your task done

Now please write an email based on your task in Part 1.

Task 4   Inquiring and Offering

LEARNING OBJECTIVE:

☞ To be able to write e-mails making general inquiries, specific inquiries & offers

Part 1   Getting to know your task

Scenario 1:

Mr. Swart, the purchasing manager[1] of Peliadora Trading Corporation, is a large dealer in beauty and personal care[2] in South Africa. He is interested in Hair Extensions and Wigs[3] produced in China. Having seen product information on www. alibaba. com, he is approaching[4] Qingdao Top Beauty Hair Products Co., Ltd. for an offer[5] for 14″ Peruvian Remy Hair Weft Body Wave[6].

Task 1:

Write an inquiry[7] to Qingdao Top Beauty Hair Products Co., Ltd. on behalf of[8] Mr. Swart to ask for price, MOQ[9], packaging[10], shipment[11], terms of payment[12] and etc. Ask them to provide catalogues[13] and samples too.

Brainstorming:

How to make an effective inquiry?

NOTES:

1. purchasing manager: 采购经理

2. beauty and personal care：美容及个人护理品

3. Hair Extensions and Wigs：接发和假发

4. approach：*v.* 联系

We have been approached by several buyers for the supply of 3D printers.

许多买家向我方联系购买 3D 打印机。

5. offer：*n.* 报盘

to make/give/send sb. an offer for/on sth.

向某人报盘某物

Please make us an offer CIF San Francisco for Sheepskin Snow Boots.

请向我方报盘羊皮雪地靴成本加运费加保费旧金山价格。

offer：*v.* 报盘

to offer sb. sth. 或 to offer sth. to sb. 向某人报盘某物

We can offer you fresh garlic at attractive prices. 我方能以具有吸引力的价格向你方报盘鲜蒜。

6. 14″ Peruvian Remy Hair Weft Body Wave：14 寸秘鲁倒顺大波浪发帘

7. inquiry：*n.* （美语）询盘，询价，询购，英语常用 enquiry

to make/send/give/sb. an inquiry for sth. 向某人询购某货

We are making you an inquiry for electric scooters.

现向你方询盘电动滑板车。

inquire：*v.* （美语）询盘，询价，询购，英语常用 enquire

We are inquiring for lawn mowers.

我们正在询盘割草机。

8. on behalf of：以……的名义，代表……

We will arrange insurance on behalf of you.

我方将代表你方办理保险。

9. MOQ：Minimum Order Quantity 最小订量，起订量

10. packaging：*n.* 包装，用法详解见 Task 8

11. shipment：*n.* 装运，用法详解见 Task 7

12. terms of payment：付款条件；支付条件，用法详解见 Task 9

13. catalogue：*n.* 产品目录

illustrated catalogue 带插图的产品目录

Scenario 2：

After receiving the inquiry from Mr. Swart, Erick Liu from Qingdao Top Beauty Hair Products Co., Ltd. is making him an offer.

1. 14″ Peruvian Remy Hair Weft Body Wave at ＄26.5/piece FOB Ningbo

2. No MOQ requirement

3. Each piece will be packed in a clean PVC bag[1] and a cardboard[2] or a customized packaging bag[3].

4. Shipment after payment by UPS, DHL or TNT

5. Payment by ESCROW, Western Union, PayPal or T/T

6. Catalogues and samples have been airmailed.

Task 2:

Write an offer to Mr. Swart on behalf of Erick Liu with the information mentioned above.

Brainstorming:

How to make a satisfactory offer?

NOTES:

1. PVC bag: 塑料袋

2. cardboard: n. 纸箱

3. customized packaging bag: 定制包装袋

Part 2   Learning about a similar task

Sample e-mail 1: An inquiry

From: dylan@ jhtrading. com. cn
To: sathida@ scg. com. th
Date: Jun. 9, 20—
Subject: An inquiry for A4 Copy Paper
Dear Sir/Madam,   We learn from www. thaipaper. com that you are a leading paper supplier in Thailand. We are a China (Qingdao) based company[1] looking for a long term partner for the product. We are very interested in your A4 Copy Paper both in Supreme and Idea series[2]. Would you please inform[3] us of the following information in detail[4]:   1. specifications[5], photos and analysis report[6] of the product   2. prices on FOB terms[7]   3. MOQ   4. packaging of the product   5. shipment   6. payment terms   7. whether the FORM E[8] can be applied for[9]?   Please confirm the above details[10]. We would appreciate[11] it if you could quote[12] us your most favorable

prices[13]. If your prices are competitive, we will place a large order[14] with you. Looking forward to your early reply.

Dylan Wang
Sales Manager
Qingdao Junhui Trading Co., Ltd.
Add.：51 Taiping Rd., Qingdao, China
Tel.：+86 − 532 − 82971888
Fax：+86 − 532 − 82971777
Website：www. junhuitrading. com

NOTES：

1. China（Qingdao）based company：位于中国(青岛)的公司

2. in... series：……系列

3. inform：*v.* 告知

（1）inform sb. of sth.

Please inform us of your earliest date of delivery.

请告知我方你们的最早交货日期。

（2）inform sb. that（what、when、why、where、how、whether 等）从句

We wish to inform you that this deal has been done at USD 80 per ton FOB Qingdao.

兹告知你方这笔交易已按每吨 80 美元，青岛装运港船上交货价。

（3）Please be informed of sth. 或 that 从句

Please be informed that we have already airmailed the samples you request.

兹告知你方，我们已经将你方所需样品空邮寄出。

Please keep us informed of any fluctuations of the prices of soybeans.

请随时通知我方大豆价格的波动情况。

4. in detail：详细地

Attached please find the catalogue of our new products in detail.

现随函寄去我方新产品的详细目录一份，请查收。

5. specification：*n.* 规格，常用复数

6. analysis report：分析报告

7. on... terms：按……条款

Thank you for your offer for 10 metric tons of Black Pepper on the usual terms.

感谢你方按惯常条款报盘 10 公吨黑胡椒。

8. FORM E：中国东盟自由贸易区优惠原产地证明书，英文名称为《ASEAN-CHINA FREE TRADE AREA PREFERENTIAL TARIFF CERTIFICATE OF ORIGIN FORM E》。

9. apply for：申请

In order to enable you to apply for the necessary Import License, we are sending you a copy of Proforma Invoice.

为了你方申请必要的进口许可证，兹寄上一份形式发票。

10. Please confirm details. 请(给我们)确认详细情况。

11. appreciate：*v.* 感谢，感激

（1）appreciate sth.

We highly appreciate your close cooperation.

我方十分感激你方的密切合作。

Your prompt reply would be highly appreciated.

如能立即答复，我方将不胜感激。

（2）appreciate（one's）doing sth.

We appreciate your making the effort to meet our request.

我方非常感谢你方为满足我们的要求而做的努力。

（3）appreciate it if...

We should appreciate it if you willreply to us at an early reply.

如能早日答复，我方将不胜感激。

（4）It will/would be appreciated if...

It would be appreciated if you could send us your catalogue and price list.

如能寄给我方产品目录和价格表，我们将不胜感激。

12. quote：*v.* 报价

Please quote your lowest price CIF Kobe.

请报你方成本加运费加保费神户最低价。

quotation：*n.* 报价

Please make/give us your lowest quotation for Travel U Shape Pillows.

请报你方 U 型旅行枕最低价。

quotation sheet 报价单

13. favorable price：优惠的价格

14. place an order：下订单

place an order with sb. for sth.：跟……下订单订购……

I will place a large order with you for 20,000 kg dried figs.

我们将向你方订购两万公斤无花果干。

Sample e-mail 2：An offer（A reply to inquiry）

From：sathida@ scg. com. th
To：dylan@ jhtrading. com. cn
Date：Jun. 10，20—
Subject：An offer
Attachment：(1)Photos. pdf (2)Specification. doc (3)Analysis report. doc

Dear Dylan,
Thank you for your inquiry of June 9, 20-- for our A4 Copy Paper both in Supreme and Idea series.

With more than 20 years' experience of handling this product, we have obtained a leading position[1] in the trade and our sales volume[2] has been increasing steadily each year. We are confident that our cooperation will bring considerable profits[3] to you.

As requested[4], we take pleasure in offering you, subject to[5] your reply reaching us by the end of this month, our A4 Copy Paper both in Supreme and Idea series as follows:

1. Supreme 70g, at USD880/MT FOB BangkokLSupreme 80g, at USD880/MT FOB Bangkok
   Idea max 70g, at USD950/MT FOB Bangkok
   Idea work 80g, at USD950/MT FOB Bangkok
2. MOQ: 6,000 PCS
3. Packaging: 500 sheets in a ream, 5 reams in a carton, 40 cartons on a pallet[6]
4. Shipment: within 20 days after receipt of relevant L/C[7]
5. Payment: by an L/C at sight or T/T 100% before production[8]
6. FORM E can be applied for.

Attached are the specifications, photos together with[9] analysis report of the product. In addition, we have airmailed you our latest catalogue. If any of the items are of interest to you, please let us know.

Your kind reply is awaited.

Best regards,
SATHIDA EUAVISALSIN
Export Manager
Thai Paper Co., Ltd.
SCG Packaging
1 Siam Cement Rd., Bangsue, Bangkok 10800, Thailand
Tel.: +66 2 586 4688
Fax: +662 586 4689
Website: www. SCGpackaging. com

NOTES:

1. leading position: 领先地位
2. sales volume: 销售量
3. considerable profits: 巨大利润
4. as requested: 根据要求
As requested, we have sent you our samples by SF Express.
按照你方的要求，我方已经用顺丰快递给你们寄去了我们的样品。
5. subject to: 以……为准，以……为条件
to 是介词，后接名词或动名词
This offer is firm subject to your reply reaching us within one week.

本报盘以你方一周之内复到有效。

6. Packaging：500 sheets in a ream, 5 reams in a carton, 40 cartons on a pallet
包装：500 张纸装一令，5 令装一个纸箱，40 个纸箱装一个托盘

7. Shipment：within 20 days after receipt of relevant L/C
装运：收到相关信用证后 20 天内安排装运

8. Payment：by an L/C at sight or T/T 100% before production
支付方式：即期信用证或生产前用电汇的方式支付全部货款

9. together with：连同……一起

Sample e-mail 3：Offering a replacement

From：viennaliu@ yongtaitrade. com
To：bakertilly@ sunrisegroup. com
Date：Sept. 25, 20--
Subject：Offer a replacement
Attachment：Price list for New model as replacement. pdf（1. 5M）

Dear Mr Baker,

　　Thank you for your e-mail of September 24, 20-- inquiring for our Self Stirring Coffee Mugs[1] Model Number ZH – 5348.

　　We regret[2] that we can no longer supply this model of self-stirring coffee mugs, which is out of production[3]. In its place we would like to offer our Self Stirring Coffee Mugs Model Number ZH – 5300 as a good replacement[4]. This is our new design, which is made of high quality stainless steel[5]. We are confident[6] that its reliable quality, exquisite workmanship and reasonable price will be satisfactory to you. The large number of repeat orders[7] we regularly receive from our customers is a clear evidence of its popularity.

　　Details of our export prices and other terms of transaction[8] are attached. Our illustrated catalogue and sample are being sent by courier[9].

　　Please keep us posted of any requirements at your end[10]. We assure[11] you that any inquiries from you will receive our prompt attention.

　　Best regards,
　　Vienna Liu
　　Marketing Manager
　　Ningbo Yongtai Trading Co., Ltd.
　　Add.：188 Changyang Road, Hongtang, Jiangbei District, Ningbo, Zhejiang, China
　　Tel.：+ 86 – 574 – 87562967
　　Fax：+ 86 – 574 – 87562967
　　Website：www. yongtaimug. com

NOTES：

1. Self Stirring Coffee Mug：自动搅拌咖啡杯

2. regret：*v.* 遗憾；抱歉

We very much regret our inability to comply with your requirements.

很抱歉，你们的要求我们无法满足。

We regret being unable to advance the shipment to early June.

很遗憾，我们无法将装运期提前到 6 月初。

We regret that you failed to make timely delivery.

很遗憾，你方未能及时交货。

n. 遗憾；抱歉

To our regret, the goods you inquired about are out of stock at present.

很抱歉，目前没有你们要的货物。

regretful：*a.* 感到遗憾的

We feel regretful that we cannot meet your request for shipment in May.

很遗憾，我们无法满足你方五月装运的请求。

regrettable：*a.* 令人遗憾的

It is regrettable that your sample quality is not up to our customers' required standard.

很遗憾，你方样品质量未达到我们客户所要求的标准。

3. out of production：不再生产

4. replacement：*n.* 调换；替代品

5. stainless steel：不锈钢

6. confident：*adj.* 有信心的，确定的

We are confident that its reliable quality, exquisite workmanship and reasonable price will be satisfactory to you.

我方相信它可靠的质量、精湛的工艺及合理的价格将令你方满意。

We feel confident that you will find the goods both excellent in quality and reasonable in price.

我方相信你方会认为这些货物品质优良，价格合理。

We are confident of the superior quality of our products.

我们对产品优越的品质有信心。

confidence *n.* 信心

This book gives me a strong sense of confidence in winning this competition.

这本书使我有了足够的信心赢得这场比赛。

7. repeat order：续订单

8. terms of transaction：交易条件

9. by courier：用快递

10.　Please keep us posted of any requirements at your end.

请随时告知我方你们的任何要求。

11.　assure：*v.* 使确信，使放心；向……保证

（1）assure sb. of sth.

We will assure you of our close cooperation at any time.

我方将确保随时与你方密切合作。

（2）assure sb that...

We assure you that we shall do our best to expedite shipment.

我方保证我们将尽全力加速装运。

（3）商业书信中还常用下面句型：

Please be assured of...（或 that 从句）请放心……

Please rest assured of...（或 that 从句）请放心……

You can be assured of...（或 that 从句）请放心……

You can rest assured of...（或 that 从句）请放心……

You can rest assured that we shall revert to your inquiry as soon as possible.

请放心，我方今后将尽速重新处理你的询盘。

Useful expressions

Making an inquiry 询盘
Expressing interest and asking for details of transaction conditions 对产品感兴趣并询问交易条件
We are interested in your Genuine Leather Belt for Men in various styles. Please send us a copy of your illustrated catalogue with details of the prices and terms of payment. 我方对不同款式的男士真皮皮带感兴趣，请寄一份带插图的产品目录并详告价格和付款方式。 We would like to buy 100 Watt Solar Panels. Please send us a detailed price list and catalogue. 我方想购买 100 瓦太阳能板。请寄给我方一份详细价目表及产品目录。 As we take interest in Bluetooth Headsets, we should be pleased if you would send us your

best quotations for Bluetooth Headphones for Running.

我方欲购蓝牙耳机，请报你方跑步用蓝牙耳机最低价。

We would like to inquire the price for 500 pieces of Disposable Facemask Item No. N201 – 9. 我方想询问你方 500 只 N201 – 9 型号一次性口罩的价格。

We should be obliged if you would give us a quotation for the supply of 200 Coffee Makers Model No. ATS – PN004.

如能向我方报 200 台 ATS – PN004 型号咖啡机的价格，我们将不胜感激。

It would also be appreciated if samples or brochure could be forwarded to us.

如果你方能寄给我方样品或小册子，我方将不胜感激。

Would you please send us some of your samples to let us know the quality and workmanship of your supplies?

你方能否寄给我方你们的一些样品使我们了解你方提供产品的质量和做工？

Stating possibility of placing an order
说明下订单的可能性

If the quality of your Canned Tuna is satisfactory and the prices acceptable, we plan to place orders in fairly large quantity.

如果你方金枪鱼罐头的质量令人满意，价格可以接受，我方将大量订购。

If your prices come up to our expectations, we would expect to place regular orders.

如果你方的价格符合我们的期望，我方将定期订购。

Should your price and delivery date be found acceptable, we will place a large order with you.

如果你方的价格和交货日期可以接受，我方将向你方大量订购。

We look forward to placing orders with you, and trust that you will make every effort to satisfy our particular requirements.

我方盼望向你方下订单并相信你方会尽最大努力满足我方的具体要求。

Making an offer 报盘

Quoting price 报价

Thank you for your inquiry of May 21 and we are pleased to send you our best quotation for Dehydrated Garlic Flakes on the basis of FOB terms.

感谢你方 5 月 21 日询盘，现高兴地向你方报脱水蒜片装运港船上交货最低价。

In reply to your inquiry dated December 10, we quote you the price CFR Rotterdam for Rattan Furniture.

现回复你方 12 月 10 日询盘，报藤条家具成本加运费鹿特丹价。

We are glad to offer you 3,000 yards of Printed Fabric at USD1. 5 per yard CIF Melbourne.

我方很高兴向你方报 3000 码印花面料，每码 1.5 美元，成本加运费加保费墨尔本。

We understand that there is a strong demand for good quality truck tyres in your market. Attached is our quotation sheet for your consideration.

我方了解到你方市场对高质量卡车轮胎需求强劲。随函附上报价单，供你方考虑。

As requested, we make an offer for the following goods.

根据你方要求，我公司就如下货物向你方报盘。

We make you the following offer subject to your reply within 10 days.

现报盘如下，以你方在 10 日之内回复为有效。

The offer is valid for 30 days.

该报盘有效期是 30 天。

Persuading customer to accept offer 说服客户接受报盘

As this product is now in great demand and the supply is rather limited, we would recommend you to accept this offer as soon as possible.

该产品目前需求量很大并且供应量十分有限，我方建议你方尽快接受该报盘。

As the prices quoted are exceptionally low and likely to rise, we would advise you to place your order without delay.

由于该报价十分低，价格有可能上涨，我方建议你方立即下订单。We trust you will find our quotation satisfactory and we look forward to receiving your order.

我方相信你方会对我方的报价感到满意，盼望收到你方的订单。

Waiting for an early reply 盼望早日回复

We look forward to your favorable and prompt reply.

盼速递佳音。

We are looking forward to hearing from you soon.

期待你方早日答复。

We thank you in advance and hope to have a prompt reply from you.

预致谢意并希望收到你方即时回复。

We shall be grateful if you will reply at an early date.

如蒙早日答复将不胜感激。

We await/anticipate/are waiting for your early reply.

期盼你方早日回复。

Your prompt reply would be highly appreciated.

如能即时回复将不胜感激。

Part 3   Getting prepared for your task

Ⅰ. Pattern drills. Make sentences with the following italicized expressions.

1. *Kindly let us know* your best quotations for bathrobes.

A. 请告诉我方成本加运费大阪价格。

B. 请告诉我方最早交货日期。

C. 请告诉我方起订量、包装及支付方式。

D. 请告诉我方你们的详细要求。

2. *We shall appreciate it if you will* quote us your lowest price for Mini Wireless Keyb-

oards.

A. 如能立即寄给我方样品，我方将不胜感激。

B. 如能寄给我方产品目录及价格单，我方将不胜感激。

C. 如能及时给我方答复，我方将不胜感激。

D. 如能报你方最优惠的价格，我方将不胜感激。

3. *If your quotation is competitive*, we will place a large order with you.

A. 如果你方报价有竞争力，我方打算订购 500 台水泵。

B. 如果你方报价有竞争力，我方将大量订购投影仪。

C. 如果你方报价有竞争力，我方将定期订购蘑菇罐头。

D. 如果你方报价有竞争力，我方有把握订购大量的台灯。

4. *We are making you an offer for* 3,000 pairs of flip flops at USD0. 6/pair FOB Fuzhou.

A. 我方现向你方报 2200 箱鱼罐头，每箱 50 美元，FOB 青岛。

B. 我方现向你方报 600 公吨小麦，每公吨 94 美元，FOB 天津。

C. 我方现向你方报 1000 打钢笔，每打 6 英镑，CFR 利物浦。

D. 我方现向你方报 600 件开衫，每件 10 美元，CIF 温哥华，含 5% 佣金。

5. *This offer is firm subject to* your reply reaching here before September 2.

A. 该报盘以你方的答复在本月底前到达我方有效。

B. 该报盘以你方的答复在一周之内到达我方有效。

C. 该报盘以你方在五月底前接受有效。

D. 该报盘以你方本月 25 日前确认有效。

Ⅱ. Put the sentences in the e-mail into a correct order. Then translate it into Chinese.

_____ We are a large dealer of Baby Clothes in Canada with more than 30 years of experience in this line.

_____ We are very interested in your Baby Pajamas and should appreciate your sending us the latest illustrated catalogues and price lists.

_____ When quoting, please state your terms of payment and discount you would allow on purchases of not less than 100 pieces of individual items.

_____ We understand from your information posted on www. alibaba. com that you are a leading exporter of Baby Pajamas in your country.

_____ If your prices are competitive, we will place bulk orders with you.

_____ Would you please send us details of various ranges, including sizes, colors and prices, and also samples of the different qualities of material used.

_____ We look forward to receiving your early reply.

Ⅲ. Read the inquiry. Then make improvements in its reply in terms of grammar, word choice and content.

An inquiry

Dear Sir/Madam,

How are you? This is Antonio from Mexico. I have my own business with kids enjoyment. I am looking for small machines like the Coin Operated Kiddie Ride you published on www. alibaba. com. Please kindly provide：

1. Catalogue with the designs and prices

2. Minimum order quantity

3. Are coins from different countries workable? Can you change the coin's size to that of my country? What is the procedure to do that?

4. How much does the shipment of one or two machines to Mexico cost?

I would appreciate your early reply in advance.

Best regards,

Antonio

A reply to the inquiry

Antonio,

Well received your inquiry with many thanks. This is Grace Zhao from guangzhou Baoli animation technology co., Ltd. Well noted that your interested in the Kiddie Ride, and enclosed you will find the Quotation for some of our items for your kindly reference. Also, pls find the attached pictures you may interested in. Minimum order quantity normally we can accept 1 piece as an sample order. Delivery time 5 days for production after receiving your deposit and about 15 days for delivery after receiving your balance. Payment term we support T/T at this stage. (i. e. 30% deposit before production and 70% balance before delivery) What's your comments for this product now? If you have any questions pls feel free to contact me. Waiting for your early reply.

Grace Zhao

Part 4 **Getting your task done**　▷ ▷ ▷

Now please write an e-mail based on your Task 1 in Part 1.

Now please write an e-mail based on your Task 2 in Part 1.

Attachment:

QUOTATION SHEET FOR TROLLEY CASE SETS

Item No.	Specifications	FOB SHANGHAI		Quantity/20FCL	Sample Photo	Carton Size
		Size	USD			
DL020	(1) Material: PC + ABS; (2) #8 Plastic zipper; (3) Retractable handles; (4) Aluminum built-in retractable trolley; (5) Four 360 degrees wheels; (6) Combination lock; (7) 210D nylon lining + pocket + elastic belts	20″24″28″	$63. 5/set	3. 1mts/20fcl About: 230 sets		3 pcs/1 set/1 carton/49x31x77 (cm)
DL030	Ditto	20″24″28″	$63. 5/set	2. 7mts/20fcl About: 200 sets		3 pcs/1 set/1 carton/52x34x78 (cm)
DL031	Ditto	20″24″28″	$62. 5/set	2. 7mts/20fcl About: 200 sets		3 pcs/1 set/1 carton/52x34x78 (cm)

续 表

Item No.	Specifications	FOB SHANGHAI Size	FOB SHANGHAI USD	Quantity/20FCL	Sample Photo	Carton Size
DL033	Ditto	20″24″28″	$63. 5/set	2. 7mts/20fcl About: 200 sets		3 pcs/1 set/1 carton/52x34x78 (cm)
DL012	(1) Material:PC + ABS; (2) #8 Plastic zipper; (3) Retractable handles; (4) Aluminum built-inretractable trolley; (5) Four 360 degrees mulit wheels; (6) Combination lock; (7) 210D nylon lining + pocket + elastic belts	20″24″28″	$65. 5/set	2. 7mts/20fcl About: 200 sets		3 pcs/1 set/1 carton/52x34x78 (cm)
DL001	(1) Material: PC + ABS; (2) #8 Plastic zipper; (3) Retractable handles; (4) Aluminum built-in retractable trolley; (5) Four 360 degrees wheels; (6) Combination lock; (7) 210D nylon lining + pocket + elastic belts	20″24″28″	$62. 5/set	2. 7mts/20fcl About: 200 sets		3 pcs/1 set/1 carton/53x34x77 (cm)

Task 5　Making a Counter-offer

Part 1　Getting to know your task

Scenario:

You are Mr. Swart of Peliadora Trading Corporation. You have received offers for Hair Extensions and Wigs from a number of suppliers in China, most of which are quoted at USD10/piece FOB terms. You are particularly interested in the products of Qingdao Top Beauty Hair Products Co., Ltd., but find their price to be USD12/piece FOB Qingdao.

Task:

Write their sales person Mr. Lu an e-mail to ask if they can bring down the price to USD10.

Brainstorming:

What would you emphasize on when you persuade the seller to cut the price?

Part 2　Learning about a similar task

Sample e-mail 1: Making a counter-offer[1] (1)

From: giwsdc@ spspa. au
To: sunfine@ vip. 163. com
Date: July 10, 20—
Subject: Re: offer for Art Bags

Dear Mike,

Thank you for your offer of July 9 for the Art Bags at USD 20/PC FOB Qingdao. After careful study, we find your price too high and out of line with[2] the prevailing market. For your information, most of the competing goods are selling[3] at a level about 10% lower than[4] yours.

Should you be prepared to lower your price[5] by about 10%, i. e. at USD18/PC, we might be able to come to terms[6].

As the competition[7] is fierce, we hope you will consider our counter-offer acceptable and send us your confirmation as soon as possible.

Best regards,
Andley

NOTES:

1. counter-offer: *v. n.* 还盘

counter-表示方向相反、相对的意思，再如：

counter-sample 对等样品   counter-signature 会签

counter-trade 对等贸易   counter-purchase 互购

to counter-offer sth at...：对……还盘价格为……

We'd like to counter-offer 1,000 suitcases at US $95/pc FOB Los Angeles.

我们愿还盘1000个手提箱，每个95美元洛杉矶船上交货价。

We'd like to counter-offer 50 Euros.

我们还价50欧元。

to make a counter-offer for sth. at...：对……还盘，价格是……

Now we'd like to make you a counter-offer for 1,000 bottles of Vitamin C at USD16 per bottle CIF Shanghai.

现在我们向你还盘1000瓶维生素C，每瓶16美元成本加运保费到上海价。

2. out of line with：与……不符，脱离……

in line with：与……一致，符合……

Though we would like to conclude a deal with you, we find your price out of line with the ruling market.

虽然我们想跟你达成交易，但我们认为你方价格脱离现行市价。

the prevailing market：现行市场

the prevailing price：现行价格，时价。其他说法还有：

the ruling price, the going price, the present price, the current price 等。

3. sell：*v.* 销售

注意很多情况下sell用主动语态表示被动意思，如：

These baskets sell well/fast in the American market.

这些篮子在美国市场上卖得非常快。

4. 10% lower than：比……低 10%

10% higher than：比……高 10%

We can't cut our prices as they are already 5% lower than quotations from our competitors.

我们不能降价，因为它们比竞争者的报价已经低出 5%。

5. lower one's price by (to)...：将某人的价格降低(至)……

类似的说法还有：

cut one's price by (to)...

reduce one's price by (to)...

bring down one's price by (to)... 等

There is not much possibility of business unless you can reduce your price by 5%.

除非你能降价 5%，否则没有太大成交希望。

6. come to terms = come to agreement：达成协议

The two sides have come to terms on the unit price of the goods.

双方就货物的单价达成一致。

7. competition：n. 竞争

Competition in the market is fierce/intense/keen.

市场竞争激烈。

competitive：a. 竞争激烈的；有竞争力的；竞争性的

Small firms are trying to find their way to survive in the competitive world of business.

小公司试图寻找出路，以在当今充满竞争的世界里生存。

competitive goods 竞争性货物，也可以说 competing goods

compete：v. 竞争

The two companies are competing against/with each other to get people to buy their goods.

这两家公司相互竞争客源。

competitor：n. 竞争者，竞争对手

We are trying to keep our new product a secret from our competitors.

对于我们的新产品，我们试图对竞争者保密。

Brainstorming：

What information could be given in a counter-offer e-mail as reasons for the reduction of price? Please tick the appropriate box(es).

☐ quantity

☐ quality

- [ ] long-term relationship
- [ ] competition
- [ ] delivery time
- [ ] exchange rate
- [ ] market situation

Sample e-mail 2：Making a counter-offer（2）

From：sunfine@ vip. 163. com
To：giwsdc@ spspa. au
Date：July 11，20——
Subject：Re：Re：offer for Art Bags
Dear Andley, Your e-mail of July 10 has been received with many thanks. We agree with you when you say that our prices are higher than those of our competing goods，but please note that our materials are carefully selected. If you compare our samples with others，you will find our products are superior[1] to most of them in the present market，and know the reasons why our clients in Europe and A-merica keep buying from us at our price level. So we do hope that you can draw your end-users[*2] attention to[3] the quality，rather than prices only. However，in view of[4] the longstanding business relations[5] between us，we are willing to reduce our price by 3%. We hope that we can strike a deal[6] at USD 19. 4/PC FOB Qingdao. Your early reply will be appreciated. Best regards, Mike Liu

NOTES：

1. superior：*a.* 比……好的，高的，优的

We can assure you that the quality of our goods is superior to any other similar products a-vailable on the present market.

我们可以保证我们货物的质量比现今市场上可以买得到的同类产品都要好。

inferior：*a.* 比……劣的，次的，低的，差的

Please always bear in mind that goods of inferior quality will find no market here.

请永远记住，劣质货在这儿是没有销路的。

2. end-user：最终用户

3. draw sb's attention to：请某人注意

还可以说成 direct/invite/call sb's attention to. . .

We would like to draw your attention to the fact that the delivery date is approaching, but we haven't received your relevant L/C so far.

我们想请你们注意，交期临近，但目前为止我们尚未收到你们的有关信用证。

4. in view of：鉴于，由于

In view of the rising tendency in the market, we'd suggest you accept our offer.

鉴于目前市场的上涨趋势，我们建议你方接受我们的报价。

5. longstanding business relations：长期的业务关系

6. strike a deal：达成交易；达成协议

达成交易还可表达为：

conclude/close/complete/finalize a deal/a transaction

Although we are desperately trying our best, we are still unable to strike a deal.

尽管我们已经竭尽全力了，我们还是未能成交。

Sample e-mail 3：Making a counter-offer（3）

From：giwsdc@ spspa. au
To：sunfine@ vip. 163. com
Date：July 12, 20--
Subject：Re：Re：Re：offer for Art Bags
Dear Mike, Thank you for your prompt reply. Your quality is good, but your price is absolutely beyond[1] what we can accept. We'd be willing to go up to[2] USD18. 6/PC. This is the best price[3] we can give you. We will not be able to strike a deal at any price higher than this. Given the declining market[4] and competition from low-price goods, your price must be very competitive if you want to push the sales of your products here. We hope our price is acceptable to you. Best regards, Andley

NOTES：

1. beyond：prep. 在……之外的；超过……的

beyond what we can accept：是我们所不能接受的

We are sorry to say that such terms of payment are beyond our financial strength.

很遗憾，这种支付条件超出了我们的财力。

2. We'd be willing to go up to . . . : 我们愿意把价格提高到……。

"提价"还可以表达为：raise/increase the price

We have raised the price by 10 dollars, and we don't think we can go up any further.

我们已经把价格提高了 10 美元，我们不能再提了。

3. best price：最好的价格（此处指最高的价格）

注意该词随说话人的角度不同而有不同的意思，可以是"最高的价格"，也可以是"最低的价格"。

4. Given the declining market：考虑到下跌的市场

given：考虑到

Given the domestic weakness, Japan might further stimulate exports in order to sustain its economic growth.

考虑到国内的疲软，日本可能会进一步刺激出口，以维持经济增长。

the declining market：下跌的市场

市场下跌还可表达为：

The market is dropping/falling/going down/weakening.

Owing to worldwide economic recession, the international market has fallen sharply.

由于世界范围的经济衰退，国际市场急剧下跌。

相反，市场上涨可表达为：

The market is rising/going up/strengthening/advancing.

Ever since we signed the last contract, prices for computer CPUs have gone up by 5%.

自从我们签订了上笔合同后，电脑处理器的价格就上涨了 5%。

Sample e-mail 4：Accepting a counter-offer（4）

From：sunfine@ vip. 163. com
To：giwsdc@ spspa. au
Date：July 13, 20—
Subject：Re：Re：Re：Re：offer for Art Bags
Dear Andley,   Thank you for your e-mail of July 12.   Considering our longstanding friendly business relations with you, we are willing to accept your price, i. e. 500PCS at USD18. 6/PC. This is really our rock bottom price[1], and we haven't done any business at a price lower this.   We believe our quality art bags will enjoy fast sales[2] at your end.   Look forward to receiving your order.   Best regards,   Mike Liu

NOTES：

1. rock bottom price：最低价

最低价还可表达为 lowest price、minimum price、floor price 等

2. enjoy fast sales：畅销

表示"畅销"通常有下列表达方法：

Our goods enjoy excellent sales.

我们的产品很畅销。

Cashmere coats always sell well.

羊绒大衣总是很畅销。

Our garments have a ready market in your region.

我们的服装在你地区销路很好。

Our goods are well received.

我们的货物很受欢迎。

This product is very marketable.

这个产品很畅销。

Useful expressions

The influence factor of price：market tendency 影响价格的因素：市场趋势
The market is firm with an upward tendency. 市场坚挺，行情看涨。 The market is strong, and the price will continue to go up. 市场坚挺，价格将继续上涨。 As the market is weak, please consider our counter-offer acceptable. 由于市场疲软，请考虑接受我们的还盘。 As the market is surging, there is much likelihood of price increasing in the near future. 由于市场大幅上涨，不久后价格将上涨的可能性很大。
The influence factor of price：competition 影响价格的因素：竞争形势
As the competition is very fierce, please lower your price by 10% so as to enable us to push the sales of your products. 由于竞争激烈，请降价10%以便我们能推销贵方产品。 The competition from low-priced goods is keen. 来自低价格商品的竞争非常激烈。
The influence factor of price：quality 影响价格的因素：质量
As the quality of our products is much better than that of others, it is understandable that our price is a little higher.

由于我们产品的质量比别的产品好得多，价格有点高是可以理解的。

Although the products of your company are superior to others, your price is too high to be acceptable.

虽然你们公司的产品比别的产品优质，但你们的价格太高难以接受。Different quality means different price.

质量不一样，因此价格也不同。

Quality is life of products.

质量是产品的生命。

The influence factor of price: quantity 影响价格的因素：数量

Your order is rather small in quantity, which makes it difficult for us to consider any reduction in our price.

你们的订单数量太小，我们很难考虑降价。

I think we deserve a better price, given the large size of our order.

考虑到我们订单数量巨大，我们应该享受更好的价格。

The influence factor of price: delivery time 影响价格的因素：交货期

As the delivery time you desired is very urgent, our factory has to work overtime to speed up the production, which adds to our cost. We find it difficult to reduce our price.

由于你们要求的交货期非常急，我们工厂需要加班来加快生产，这增加了我们的成本。我们很难来降低价格。

The influence factor of price: cost 影响价格的因素：成本

As the labor costs have gone up by 10%, there is no room for us to lower the price.

由于劳动成本已经上涨了10%，对我们来说已没有降价的空间。

As the materials of the products have dropped by 10%, we expect you to cut your price accordingly.

由于产品原材料价格已经下跌了10%，我们期待你方能相应地降低价格。

As Renminbi has appreciated remarkably against the US dollar, it is difficult for us to maintain our low price level of the past.

因为人民币对美元大幅升值，我们很难维持过去的低价水平。

Non-acceptance of prices 不接受价格

Your price is so high to accept that it would leave us little profit.

你们的价格太高了，接受这个价格几乎给我们没有留下什么利润。

We feel regretful that we can't accept your offer.

很遗憾不能接受你方报盘。

It's regrettable that we have to decline your counter-offer.

很遗憾我们必须拒绝你方还盘。

Your price is much higher than what we can accept.

你方价格远高于我们所能接受的范围。

Your price is far beyond our expectations.

你方价格(之高)远远超乎我们的意料。
Your price is far beyond reasonable.
你方价格太不合理。

Asking for/declining/making concessions 要求让步、无法让步，同意让步

If you can't reduce your price by 5%, we have to place our order elsewhere.
如果贵公司不能降价5%，我们只能别处订购。
We hope our counter offer is acceptable to you, and shall place regular orders with you in the future.
我们希望贵公司能同意我们的还盘，将来我们将从你方定期订购。
In order to push the sales of your products more efficiently, I suggest that you bring down your price by 5%. 为了更好地推销你们产品，我们建议你方降价5%。As our products are in heavy demand, we are sorry that we can't meet your request for reducing the price.
由于我们的产品需求量巨大，抱歉不能接受你方降价的请求。
As we have quoted you our best price, it's difficult for us to consider any reduction.
由于我们已向你方报出我们最优惠的价格，很难再考虑任何降价。
The best we can do is to make a reduction of 5% in our previous quotation.
我们最多能在我们先前的报价中降价5%。
In order to establish long-standing business relations with you, we'd like to reduce our price to USD10 per piece.
为了与贵方建立长期的业务关系，我方愿意把价格降低到每件10美元。
In order to facilitate your sales, we are willing to accept your counter-offer.
为了便于你方销售，我们愿意接受你方还盘。

Part 3　Getting prepared for your task

Ⅰ. Pattern drills. Make sentences with the following italicized expressions.

1. *For your information*, we have attached our latest price list.

A. 供你方参考，你方价格比其他供应者的价格高10%。

B. 供你方参考，别的买家一直按我方报价长期订购。

C. 供你方参考，我们的目标价为每件10美元。

D. 供你方参考，你方的价格远远超出了我们的预期。

2. *In view of* the longstanding relationship between us, we'd like to reduce our price.

A. 鉴于目前市场行情上涨的趋势，我们很难降价销售。

B. 鉴于你方订单数量太少，我们很难把价格降到5美元一件。

C. 鉴于目前市场供大于求，请你们调整价格，以便更好地销售。

D. 鉴于你方上涨的价格，我们不得不转向其他供应商。

3. *Please note that* our materials are carefully selected.

A. 请注意别的供应商的价格比你方的低 10%。

B. 请注意交货期临近。

C. 请注意我们报盘的有效期为 7 天。

D. 请注意别的买家在按照我们的报价大量购买。

4. *Considering/Given* our long-standing business relations, we give you a special discount.

A. 考虑到你方订单数量较大，我们愿意接受你方还盘。

B. 考虑到这是你我之间的第一笔交易，我们愿意降价 2%。

C. 考虑到近期上涨的行市，我们建议你方尽快接受我们的报价。

D. 考虑到你方产品的优良品质，我们愿意订购 500 件。

Ⅱ. Translate the following sentences into Chinese.

1. Your price is so high to accept that it would leave us with too small a margin of profit.

2. We think that a reduction of 5% may facilitate a conclusion of the business.

3. We admit that the quality of your products is slightly better than others, but the difference in price should, in no case, be as big as 10%.

4. As the labor cost has gone up recently, it's difficult for us to strike a deal at the previous price.

5. We hope this counter offer will meet with your approval and we shall place regular orders in the future.

Ⅲ. Fill in the blanks with proper forms of the following words.

| compete | competition | competitive | competitor | competing |

1. You will be _____ with the best companies in the world.

2. You are too small to _____ with a company like that.

3. Speaking of quality, our products are among the best ones, and can stand the keenest _____ anywhere at any time.

4. As our sole agent, you are not allowed to handle any _____ products in your region within the duration of the agreement.

5. China is also trying to build up its expertise in cars and machinery and becoming a _____ as well as a customer.

Ⅳ. Translate the following e-mail into Chinese:

Dear Chris,

Thank you for your e-mail of May 1.

To be frank, our production cost has gone up by 10% because of the rise in the labor costs and the appreciation of Renminbi Yuan. Therefore, we regret to say that we are unable to accept your price at USD7. 80/piece.

However, if you can increase your quantity to 5,000 pieces, we may consider allowing you a special discount of 5%.

Waiting for your early confirmation.

Best wishes,
Joy

Part 4　Getting your task done

Now please write an e-mail based on your task in Part 1.

Task 6　Making a Counter Sample

LEARNING OBJECTIVE:

☞ To be able to write e-mails to handle sample issues

Part 1　Getting to know your task

Scenario 1:

Tracy, Sales Director of Carters Trading Company in Nanjing, has received two purchase samples[1] of decorative stainless steel flowers[2] from a European client, who asks for 4 counter samples[3] for each one. After discussing with technicians[4], she knows that two new molds[5] need to be made for production of counter samples, which will cost USD 500 respectively.

The buyer's details follows below:

Name: Alfa Laval Oy

Address: Luoteisrinne 4 C, FI 02270, Espoo, Finland

E-mail: info. aloyfi@ alfalaval. com

Contacts: Watt

Task 1:

Write an e-mail to confirm receipt of the purchase samples and negotiate with them about the mold fees.

Scenario 2:

Carters Trading Company has received the mold fees from Alfa and made 4 counter samples for each purchase sample and sent two of them to the client for their confirmation by FedEx[6] with tracking number[7] 546781078429 and kept the remaining[8] two pieces as duplicate samples[9].

Task 2:

Write an e-mail to inform the tracking number, ask for confirmation of the counter samples and purchase order from Alfa.

Brainstorming：

What will happen if your counter samples fail to reach the requirements?

NOTES：

1. purchase sample：购货样品，是指买方寄给卖方的所要购买的产品，用来制作复制样品

2. decorative stainless steel flowers：不锈钢装饰花

3. counter sample：回样；对等样品

在实际贸易业务中，如卖方认为按买方来样供货没有切实把握，卖方可根据买方来样仿制或从现有货物中选择品质相近的样品提交买方。

4. technician：技术员、技师

5. mold：*n.* 模具

6. FedEx：联邦快递公司

7. tracking number：追踪号码；运单号，联邦快递单号一般是 12 位数字

8. remaining：*adj.* 剩余的

The remaining issues can be dealt with in the next meeting.

剩余事项下次会议再处理。

9. duplicate sample：复样，也称留样

向买方送交样品时，卖方应留存的一份或数份同样的样品。

Part 2 Learning about a similar task

Sample e-mail 1：Confirming receipt of purchase samples

From：James_Brown@ TM. NET. MY
To：Mary_Green@ triple-r. com. hk
Subject：Re：purchase samples
Attachment：Pictures of purchase sample. pdf(1. 5M)
Dear Mary,   We have received your purchase sample Art. No. EED2145 with many thanks.   We are pretty sure that we could make the counter samples to your satisfaction and will send them to you within 10 days by DHL[1].

After discussing with our technicians, we know that we will make a new mold for production of your sample, which costs USD 390. Please pay for mold fees before our production. As a rule, we will start production as soon as we receive your payment.

We look forward to your favorable reply.

Best regards,

Brown

NOTES：

1. DHL：敦豪快递

Sample e-mail 2：Confirming sending the samples and notifying the tracking number

From：Black_Berry_Smith@ terseed. com
To：Floyd_Schrock@ yatex. com
Subject：tracking number
Dear Floyd, We are glad to tell you that we have made four counter samples, which are in exact conformity with[1] your purchase sample. Two of them have been sent to you by DHL with its tracking No. 6705025471, the remaining two pieces have been kept as duplicate samples by us. We hope our samples will be satisfactory[2] to you, and are looking forward to your purchase order. Best regards, Berry Smith

NOTES：

1. in conformity with. . . :与……完全相符，与……完全一致

Decisions must be taken in conformity with the company's procedures.

公司决策必须完全符合公司程序。

To avoid any possible complaint, we wish to make it clear that the goods supplied must be in conformity with the samples in both quality and design.

为避免任何可能的异议，我们想说明供给我们的货物在品质和设计上必须与样品完全一致。

还可以说：

be in accordance with. . .

be in compliance with. . .

be in line with. . .

be in agreement with. . .

be in correspondence with. . .

conform to vi. 符合；遵照；适应环境

Before buying the baby's car seat, make sure that it conforms to the official safety standards.

购买婴儿车之前，要确保它符合官方的安全标准。

Members have to conform to a strict dress code.

成员们必须遵守严格的着装规定。

还可以说：

accord with. . .

comply with. . .

correspond with/to. . .

2. satisfactory：*adj.* 令人满意的

If the price of your products is satisfactory, we shall be able to place substantial orders with you.

如果你方产品的价格令人满意，我们将能够向你方大量订购。

satisfied：adj. 感到满意的

be satisfied with. . .：对……感到满意

We are not satisfied with your quotation. It is apparently out of line with the market.

我们对你方报价不满意，它显然和市价不符。

satisfaction：*n.* 满意

If the first shipment turns out to the satisfaction of our customers, we will place repeat orders with you.

如果首批货物令我方客户满意，我们将向你方续订。

satisfy：*v.* 使满意

The patterns of your carpets satisfy us. We will order 1,000 pieces.

你方地毯的图案使我们很满意。我们将订购 1000 件。

Useful expressions

Making samples 制作复样
We will make counter samples on receipt of your sample fees. 一收到贵方样品费，我方立即制作回样。 Samples will be ready/finished/completed within 3 days. 样品将在三天内完成。 Please do sampling as quickly as possible, as we have to show them at the coming Dubai Fair. 请尽快打样，我们要在即将举办的迪拜交易会上推出。

We will let you know about sampling status.

我们会让您知道样品的进展情况。

We are sending you by airmail samples of our products, which will certainly give you all the details you need.

我们空邮寄给你方产品样品，这些样品会展示所有需要的细节。

Please do the sampling based on our three-color logo as attached.

请根据附件中我们的三色图标打样。

We have made the counter samples strictly corresponding to your purchase sample.

我们已制作与购货样品完全一致的回样。

Confirming samples 确认样品

We are eager to get your approval for samples.

我非常需要您对于样品的确认。

We hope our counter samples could match your request.

希望我们的回样能达到贵方的要求。

We have received your counter samples and find them satisfactory.

我们已经收到你们的回样，对其表示满意。

Part 3 Getting prepared for your task

Ⅰ. Pattern drills. Make sentences with the following italicized expressions.

1. *We have received* your *purchase sample* Art. No. EED2145 *with many thanks.*

A. 我们已经收到你方货号为 AD134、AD135 和 AD136 的购货样品，非常感谢。

B. 我们已经收到了你方的回样，非常感谢。

C. 我们已经收到了你方泰迪熊毛绒玩具购货样品，非常感谢。

D. 我们已经收到了你方制作的假发回样，非常感谢。

2. We are glad to tell you that we have made four counter samples, which are *in exact conformity with* your purchase sample.

A. 根据要求，我们制作了与你方购货样品完全一致的回样。

B. 请注意你方的供货要与购货样品的质量和色泽完全一致。

C. 我们很抱歉的告知贵方所提供的货物尺寸与购货样品不一致。

D. 货物标识要与我们提供的标识完全一致。

3. Two of them have been sent to you *by DHL* with its *tracking No.* 6705025471.

A. 我们今天会将回样通过联邦快递寄出，追踪号为 492086852522.

B. 今天上午我们已经通过邮政特快专递(EMS)寄出回样，追踪号为 CN736292937。

C. 我们已经通过美国邮政快递(USPS)Priority mail 寄出购货样品，预计 7 天能到达贵方，追踪号为 CW283042525US。

D. 回样已经由美国快递公司(UPS)寄出，跟踪号为 1ZY01Y240408665148。

II. Fill in the blanks with the correct words.

satisfactory   satisfy   satisfied   satisfaction

1. If the first order turns out to be an entire _____ to us, we will order with you in large quantities.

2. Actually, we are not quite _____ with the goods you supplied, because the color is obviously different from our purchase sample.

3. We hope our new product will be _____ to you.

4. We are _____ with your shipment and believe they will enjoy excellent sales in our market.

5. If the quality and price _____ us, we will send you our purchase samples ASAP.

III. Rewrite the sentences with the noun phrases of the italicized verb phrases.

1. The counter samples we made *accord with* your purchase samples strictly.

_____

2. The stipulations in the L/C should *conform to* the terms in our contract.

_____

3. The logo design in your counter samples should *comply with* the pictures attached in last e-mail.

_____

4. Your expenses should *accord with* your incomes.

_____

5. Although the mold does not *correspond to* any criteria, it is frequently used in practice.

_____

IV. Translate the following e-mail into Chinese:

Dear Ason,

We are glad to receive your samples with many thanks.

Our factory is making the counter samples, but we can't find exactly the same button as your purchase samples. Can we substitute it with similar ones that we could find? The pictures of the replacement buttons are attached.

Please let us know your decision ASAP so as to enable us to finish producing counter samples quickly.

Best wishes,

Eric

Part 4　Getting your task done

Now please write an e-mail based on your Task 1 in Part 1.

Now please write an e-mail based on your Task 2 in Part 1.

Task 7　Discussing Time and Mode of Shipment

LEARNING OBJECTIVES:

☞ To be able to write e-mails to negotiate time and mode of shipment
☞ To be able to write e-mails to handle air shipping issues

Part 1　Getting to know your task

Scenario:

Ellen Zhang, Sales Director in Qingdao Fashion Ornaments[1] Co., Ltd. has made an offer for 5,000 pcs of Women's Crystal Brooch[2] Item No. B01M1 to Bella, who accepts all the terms and conditions[3] in this offer except the time of shipment. She asks for an earlier shipment in mid-May instead of the end of June offered.

Task 1:

Write an e-mail on behalf of Bella, asking for shipment before mid-May.

Task 2:

Write an e-mail on behalf of Ellen, suggesting making partial shipments[4] in two equal lots in May and June respectively.

Brainstorming:

What are the strengths and weaknesses of partial shipments?

NOTES:

1. ornament：装饰品；首饰
2. brooch：胸针；饰针
3. terms and conditions：条款与条件，合同条款的正式说法
4. partial shipments：分批装运

Part 2　Learning about a similar task

Sample e-mail 1：Buyer inquiring about time of shipment

From：peterson@ gmail. com
To：Cindywang@ sina. com
Subject：Time of shipment
Dear Cindy， We would like to inform you that we have persuaded our customers to accept your prices. However，they expect shipment[1] no later than mid-March in order to catch the coming selling season. We should be obliged[2] if you would take our customers' request into account[3]. Your prompt reply will be highly appreciated. Best regards， Peterson

NOTES：

1. shipment：*n.* 装运

mode of shipment 运输方式

time of shipment 装运时间

port of shipment 装运港

to effect/make shipment 装运

to advance shipment 提前装运

shipping：*a.* 装运的，运输的

shipping mark 运输标志，唛头

shipping advice 装运通知

shipping instruction 装运要求

shipping space 舱位

shipping agent/forwarding agent/forwarder 运输代理，货代

shipping company 运输公司

shipper：*n.* = consignor 托运人

2. We should be obliged if you would . . .：如蒙……，我们将不胜感激。

be obliged：感激；感谢，经常用来表示请求。

We shall be obliged if you could make timely shipment.

如果你能及时装运，我们将不胜感激。

3. take sth. into account = take sth. into consideration 考虑，考虑到

We hope you could take the above into consideration and let us know your decision.

希望你们能考虑上述内容，尽快告知我方你们的决定。

Sample e-mail 2：A reply to the above e-mail

From：cindywang@ sina. com
To：Peterson@ gmail. com
Subject：Re：Time of shipment
Dear Peterson,   After receiving your e-mail asking for delivery in mid-March, we immediately contacted our manufacturer. But to our regret, we were informed that production could only be completed in early April.   In this case, to meet your demand[1], we suggest shipping the goods in two lots[2]. The first half of the goods will be forwarded before March 15 and the second half before Apr. 10. This is the best we can do as our manufacturer is really fully committed[3] at the moment.   Your understanding will be highly appreciated and we look forward to your order.   Best regards,   Cindy

NOTES：

1. meet your demand：满足你方的需求

meet：满足，符合

meet your needs/requirements 满足你方的要求

We hope our quotation will meet your requirements and look forward to your purchase order soon.

希望我们的报价能满足你方要求并诚盼能尽快收到贵方订单。

2. ship...in 2 lots：分 2 批交货

分批装运(partial shipment)的表示方法还有：

in one lot 一次性交货

in...lots（parcels, shipments, installments)分……批交货

in...equal monthly installments of...each, beginning from...

分……批按月等量；交货，每月……（数量），从……（时间）开始

As agreed, goods are to be shipped in three equal monthly installments of 50, 000 sets each, beginning from April.

按照约定，货物将从 4 月份开始，分 3 批按月等量装运 50000 台。

3. be fully committed：承接订单太多

As we are fully committed, we are not in a position to deliver 1,000 sets of Haier Air Conditioners before the end of June。

由于承约太多，我方不能在 8 月底前交付 1000 台海尔空调。

Sample e-mail 3：Selecting a faster shipping

From：Billliu@ 126. com
To：Alfredblinder@ hotmail. com
Subject：Express Service
Dear Alfred,   As for the shipping company, we prefer FedEx to ePacket[1] for 200 wigs we have ordered from you. E-packet usually takes much longer than expected. I'd rather pay extra for shipping via FedEx. My FedEx account is：19642384 − 2.   As the goods are in urgent need, please send them tomorrow and inform us of the tracking number ASAP.   Best wishes, Bill

NOTES：

1. ePacket：2012 年 3 月，全球速卖通平台与中国邮政速递物流有限公司正式合作，为速卖通平台卖家提供更具性价比的轻小件物流服务——国际 e 邮宝。

Useful expressions

Shipment 装运
We expect to ship the balance of 15 tons by the first available steamer next month.   我们打算将剩余的 15 吨由下月第一艘便轮装运。   There is no direct steamer sailing to/for your port.   没有驶往你方港口的直达轮。   The goods have been loaded on board S. S. Red Star, which is due to sail from Qingdao to Copenhagen on or about April 7.   货物已装到红星轮上，该轮定于 4 月 7 号左右由青岛开往哥本哈根。   All the direct vessels, either liners or tramps, sailing for your port have been fully booked up.   驶往你方港口的直达轮，不管是不定期船还是班轮，都已经预订满了。
Transshipment 转运
Owing to congestion, we failed to book the necessary freight space on the designated steamer.   由于舱位拥挤，我们未能在指定的船上订到舱位。   In order to make punctual delivery, we intend to transship the goods at Macao.   为了准时交货，我们打算在澳门转船。   As direct steamers to your port are few and far between, please allow transshipment at Hong Kong.   由于到你港的直达船稀少，请允许在香港转船。
Partial shipments 分批装运
12000 sets of Fridges are to be shipped in four equal monthly installments of 3,000 sets each, beginning from March.   12000 台冰箱分四批按月等量装运，每月 3000 台，从 3 月开始。   The goods will be shipped in 2 equal installments of 20,000 m/t each, starting from June.   货物分两批等量装运，每批装 20000 公吨，从 6 月开始。   If you desire an earlier delivery, we can only make partial shipments of 10 sets in September, and the remaining 10 sets in October.   如果你方想早点交货，我们只能分批装运，9 月份 10 台，10 月份装余下的 10 台。
Air shipping service 空运
We have dispatched your package by ePacket, which will arrive in 7 days. We sincerely hope that you will give our products and services positive feedback and five-star appraisal.   货物已由国际 e 邮宝寄出，预计 7 天后到达。我们真诚地希望你可以给我们的产品和服务五星好评。   The recipient is informed that the door-to-door delivery is cancelled during holidays.   通知收件人，假日期间取消送货上门服务。   If your order is sent by DHL, sometimes it may be detained at the Customs.

如果发 DHL，有时货物会滞留海关。

If it is sent by China Post Air Mail，will the Customs in your country open the packet to check?

如果发中国航空小包，贵国海关会开包检验吗？

The postage cost depends on the weight of the package and the destination country.

邮费取决于货物重量以及目的国家。

Part 3 Getting prepared for your task

Ⅰ. Pattern drills. Make sentences with the following italicized expressions.

1. The direct steamer is due to *sail from Qingdao to Long Beach* on or before June 1.

A. 从青岛起航驶往哥本哈根港。

B. 从上海起航开往旧金山港。

C. 从大连起航驶往釜山港。

D. 从宁波起航开往阿姆斯特丹港。

2. We will *transship the goods at Hong Kong.*

We will *ship the goods via Hong Kong.*

A. 在日本横滨港转运。

B. 在葡萄牙里斯本港转运。

C. 在新加坡港转运。

D. 在澳大利亚墨尔本港转运。

3. We can make shipment *in 3 equal monthly installments* (*lots*, *shipments*, *parcels*) *of* 2,000 *pieces each*, *beginning from September.*

A. 分 3 批按月等量装运，每月装 1000 箱，从 2015 年 1 月份开始。

B. 分 4 批按月等量装运，每月装 5000 件，从 2016 年 7 月份开始。

C. 装运从 2017 年 8 月份开始，分 3 批按月等量装，每批 2000 套。

D. 装运从 2016 年 10 月份开始，分 4 批按月等量装，每批 1000 公吨。

Ⅱ. Fill in the blanks with variations of the word *ship.*

1. Goods will be _____ in 3 equal monthly lots of 50 tons each, beginning from May.
2. We will have our goods _____ by the first available steamer next month.
3. _____ is to be effected during October.
4. All the _____ space has been booked up till the end of November.
5. The _____ will be liable for any damage resulting from inadequacy or delay in delivery of such documents.

III. The following picture shows part of an express mail package cover. Read it and choose the best answer based on the information you can find on it.

1. Who is the sender?

A. Jessica Quinn   B. Liu Lunyong

C. Andy Peter

2. Who is the receiver?

A. Jessica Quinn   B. Liu Lunyong

C. Andy Peter

3. Where is the final destination city?

A. Qingdao, China   B. Lake Forest, USA

C. Los Angeles, USA

4. What is the postal code for the destination city?

A. 60045   B. 28405

C. 90015

5. What is the name of the commodity?

A. Paint Brush   B. Wig

C. Bracelet

IV. Translate the following e-mail into Chinese.

Dear Johnson,

We agree to advance shipment for 80% of the goods to November.

But after checking with the shipping company, we were informed that all the direct vessels, either liners or tramps, sailing for your port have been fully booked up till the end of November.

In this case, I think November shipment is only possible if transshipment is allowed at Hong Kong. In spite of it, it is still uncertain whether the goods will reach the bonded warehouse earlier than your expected time.

Please take the above into consideration and kindly let me know your decision soon.

Best regards,
Lily

Part 4 Getting your task done

Now please write an e-mail based on your Task 1 in Part 1.

Write a reply e-mail based on your Task 2 in Part 1.

Task 8　Packaging Arrangement

Part 1　Getting to know your task

Scenario:

Yangchun Tea Co., Ltd, a leading tea exporter in China, receives an order of 2,000 kgs Green Tea from a Czechic[1] company Co., Ltd.[2]. Anirban Ray, Sales Manager of OEZ Co., Ltd, emphasizes the importance of packaging in his last e-mail because Green Tea is likely to get spoiled from dampness in transit. In order to ensure the quality of the tea, he insists on adding a damp-proof lining in each carton.

Task:

Write an e-mail to your client Anirban Ray to identify your packaging arrangement in detail as pictured below.

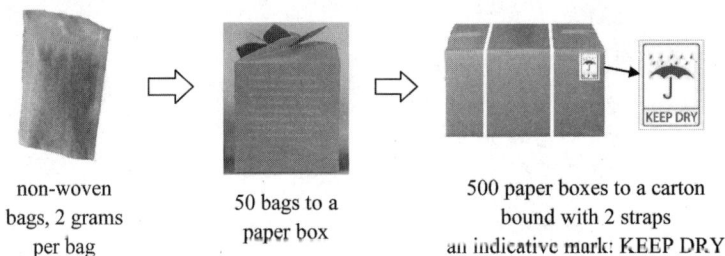

non-woven
bags, 2 grams
per bag

50 bags to a
paper box

500 paper boxes to a carton
bound with 2 straps
an indicative mark: KEEP DRY

Brainstorming:

What kinds of containers do you think are widely used in packaging of commodities in international trade?

NOTES:

1. Czechic: 捷克的

2. Co., Ltd.：有限公司称作 limited company，用在名称则用 Co., Ltd.

Part 2　Learning about a similar task ▷▷ ▷▷ ▷▷

Sample e-mail 1：Packaging arrangement

From：sunada@ allhair. com
To：tracytree@ petersoninc. com
Subject：packaging arrangement
Dear Tracy， We would like to offer you two options of packaging[1] as follows： (1) We will have each item of Indian Hair packed[2] in one transparent poly bag[3], then to a paper box, which is subject to[4] an extra cost of 9 cents. The dimensions[5] of the box are 13cm high, 15cm wide and 15cm long. Each item has a hang tag[6] and a bar code[7]. or (2)Each item of Indian Hair is packed in a transparent poly bag without cardboard carton and has a hang tag and bar code. Please tell us which of the above suits you. If you have your own requirement covering packaging, please also let us know. Best wishes， Ada

NOTES：

1. packaging：adj. 包装的

packaging arrangement 包装安排

packaging instruction 包装指示

packaging n. 包装

inner packaging 内包装

neutral packaging 中性包装

outer packaging 外包装

2. pack：v. 包装

to be packed in...of... each，... to/in... .

用某容器包装，每个容器装……，……小容器装于一大容器中。

Pens are packed in boxes of a dozen each，100 boxes to a wooden case.

钢笔要用盒装，每盒装一打，100 盒装一木箱。

Each romper suit is to be packed in a polybag, 200 pcs to a carton.

每件婴儿连体衣装一个塑料袋，200 件装一个纸板箱。

3. transparent poly bag：透明塑料袋

4. be subject to：包含，以……为条件

This price is subject to THC and BAF.

此价格含港杂费和燃油附加费。

5. dimension：*n.* 物品的长、宽或高

The dimensions of the carton are 100mm by 60mm by 60mm.

外箱尺寸为长度 10 厘米，宽度 6 厘米，高度 6 厘米。

6. hang tag：吊牌，指挂在产品上用以说明材料、规格产品的牌子或公司联系方式等信息的纸质或是 PVC 的标牌。

7. bar code：条形码

Sample e-mail 2：Packaging and shipping marks

From：billywarmer@ yahoo. com
To：cindybright@ google. com
Subject：packaging and shipping marks
Dear Cindy, As requested, we will make the following arrangements concerning packaging and shipping marks： Romantic Rose Pillar[1] Wax Candles are to be packed in boxes of half dozen each, pink, white and red equally assorted[2] with a cardboard tray[3] inside each box, 20 boxes to a cardboard carton. All the cartons are lined with[4] heat-proof[5] paper, bound with double straps[6] outside. Shipping mark[7] will consist of your initials[8], PO number and port of destination. In addition, indicative mark[9] "Keep Away From Boiler"[10] will be indicated on the upper left hand corner[11] of two long length sides[12] of the carton. Please let us know if you have other requirements. Best wishes, Billy

NOTES：

1. pillar：*n.* 柱子，支柱

2. equally assorted：平均搭配

We are pleased to order 1,000 dozen silk skirts, pink, blue, beige and yellow equally assorted.

我们高兴地订购一千打丝裙，粉、蓝、卡其色和黄平均搭配。

assortment：*n.* 搭配

Please pack our men's gloves in cartons of 60 dozen each, with equal assortment of S, M and L sizes.

男式手套请用纸箱包装，每箱60打，大、中、小号平均搭配。

3. cardboard tray：*n.* 纸板托盘

4. be lined with：内衬

Cotton Embroidered Table Cloth is packed in cartons lined with damp-proof paper.

纯棉绣花桌布用内衬防潮纸的纸箱包装。

lining：*n.* 内衬

The case has tin-plate lining.

这个箱子内衬锡箔。

5. heat -proof：*adj.* 防热的

类似的表达方式还有：

damp-proof 防潮的　　　　　　water-proof 防水的

shock-proof 防震的　　　　　　wind-proof 防风的

fire-proof 防火的　　　　　　　moth-proof 防蛀的

air-tight 密封的　　　　　　　rust-resistant 不生锈的

6. bound with double straps outside 外面用两根袋子捆住

strap：*n.* 打包带

bound 是 bind(*v.* 捆，绑)的过去分词

加固包装的表达方式通常有：

We would suggest you strengthen the carton with double straps.

我们建议用两道打包带加固纸板箱。

The goods must be packed in strong wooden cases secured with iron hoops at both ends.

货物须以结实的木箱包装，两端用铁箍加固。

We do not object to packing in cartons, provided the flaps are glued down and cartons reinforced with metal bands.

如果盖子被粘牢而且箱子用金属带加固，我们不反对用纸板箱包装。

7. shipping mark：运输标志，装船唛头

内容主要包括：收货人或买方名称的英文缩写字母或简称、参考号，如运单号、订单号或发票号、目的地名称和货物件数。

8. initial：*n.* 起首的字母；initials（pl.）名字的起首字母缩写

VOA = Voice of America 美国之声

WTO = World Trade Organization 世界贸易组织

MIT = Massachusetts Institute of Technology 麻省理工学院

9. indicative mark：指示性标志

按商品的特点，对于易碎、需防湿、防颠倒等商品，在包装上用醒目图形或文字，标明"小心轻放"、"防潮湿"、"此端向上"等。指示性标志用来指示运输、装卸、保管人员在作业时需要注意到事项，以保证物资的安全。这种标志主要表示物资的性质，物资堆放、开启、吊运等的方法。

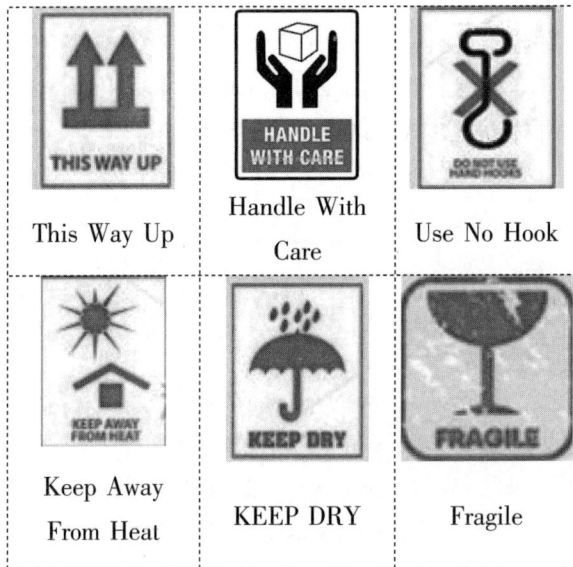

| This Way Up | Handle With Care | Use No Hook |
| Keep Away From Heat | KEEP DRY | Fragile |

warning mark：警告性标志

警告性标志又称危险品标志，是指在爆炸品、腐蚀性物品、易燃品、放射性物品、有毒品的运输包装上表明其危险性质的文字或图形说明。

| Explosive | Corrosive | Flammable | Radioactive | Poison |

Warning marks should also be stenciled on the outer packaging.

警告性标志也应刷在外包装上。

10. Keep Away From Boiler：远离锅炉

11. upper left hand corner：在左上角

upper right hand corner：右上角

12. long length side：长边

short length side：短边

Useful expressions

Packaging symbols 包装标识
Indicative marks should be stenciled in a distinctive place of the carton, such as "Handle With Care" and "This Way Up". 指示性标识如 Handle With Care、This Way Up 应刷在醒目位置。 Please stencil the shipping mark as per the drawing given. 请按所给的图样在纸板上刷唛头。 Each package should be marked "Fragile". 每件包装上应标明"易碎品"。
Packaging method 包装方式
Packaging in sturdy wooden cases is essential. Cases must be nailed, battened and secured with overall metal strapping. 用坚固木箱包装很重要。箱子须钉牢、加上压条并通体用金属带加固。 Each set of electric cooker is packed in a cardboard carton padded with formed plastic. 每台电饭锅装一纸板箱，内垫泡沫塑料。 Please note that your packaging must be able to withstand the long sea voyage. 请注意你们的包装要经得起长时间海运。
Packaging information 包装信息
No country name or company label is to appear on the outer cartons. 外箱上不允许出现国家名和公司标志。 Gross weight, net weight and tare weight are marked onto two short length sides. 在两个短边面上标注毛重、净重和皮重。
Packaging containers 包装容器
Peanuts are packed in double gunny bags. 花生用双层麻袋包装。 Each Fuji apple will be covered with plastic mesh net. One dozen should be put in a cardboard paper tray, 2 dozen to a carton with plastic paper covering on the top of apples. 每个富士苹果套一个塑料网套。每打装一个硬纸板托盘，2 打装一个纸板箱上面覆盖一块塑料纸。 20 pieces of cigarette are packed in a cigarette case lined with tin foil paper with a BOPP film outside. 20 根香烟装一个锡箔纸烟盒外加 BOPP 膜。

Part 3　Getting prepared for your task

Ⅰ. Pattern drills. Make sentences with the following italicized expressions.

1. Romantic Rose Pillar Wax Candles *are to be packed* in boxes of half dozen each.

A. 茶叶每25克装入一个密封塑料袋（air-tight PE bags），然后装入一铁盒。

B. 可口可乐345克装一听，24听装一盒。

C. 每件休闲外套装一个塑料袋，5件装一个纸板箱。

D. 每个富士苹果套一个塑料网（plastic mesh net），一打装一个纸板托盘（cardboard paper tray）。

2. All the cartons *are lined with* heat-proof paper.

All the cartons *have* heat-proof paper *linings*.

A. 玻璃杯用纸板箱包装内衬防震瓦楞纸（corrugated paper）。

B. 男士衬衫内衬防水纸。

C. 茶叶用纸板箱包装内衬防潮纸。

D. 每件羊绒大衣（cashmere coat）内衬丝绸。

3. All the cartons are *bound* with double straps.

A. 请用两条铁箍加固木箱。

B. 请用塑料打包带加固纸板箱。

C. 木箱两端请用金属条加固。

D. 每个纸盒用两条打包带加固。

Ⅱ. Fill in the blanks with the appropriate words as below.

pack	repacked	packing	package	packed	packaging

1. Please see to it that the _____ is suitable for a long sea voyage.

2. All the canned fruits and meat are to be _____ in cartons.

3. We _____ our shirts in plastic-lined, waterproof cartons, reinforced with metal straps.

4. It was found upon examination that nearly 20% of the _____ had been broken, obviously attributed to improper _____.

5. A thorough examination showed that the broken kegs were due to improper _____ for which the suppliers should be definitely responsible.

6. We can meet your requirement to have the goods _____ in wooden cases but you have to bear the extra _____ charges.

7. The goods had been _____ before they were delivered to our customers.

8. Our fountain pens are _____ in boxes of one dozen each, 100 boxes to a carton lined with water-proof paper.

9. When _____, please take into account that the boxes are likely to receive rough handling at this end and must be able to withstand transport over very bad roads.

10. You know that the appearance of the ＿＿＿＿ contributes greatly to the sale of the consumer goods.

Ⅲ. Please translate the following packaging instructions into Chinese.

PLC Label

PLC is an acronym for Packing Method, Label Name and Country Code. This label shall be placed in the upper left corner of each carton in accordance with allowance as pictured in Diagram 5 and Diagram 6. The PLC Label may be printed on a sticker and attached to the carton or printed directly onto the carton.

Part 4 ＼ Getting your task done

Now please write an e-mail based on your task in Part 1.

Task 9　Terms of Payment

Part 1　Getting to know your task

Scenario:

You have received an e-mail from an old customer as below:

From: grant@ kxt. com
To: maryyang@ yatax. com
Date: Mar. 8, 20--
Subject: T/T[1] payment terms[2]
Dear Mary,   About the payment terms for the present deal, we regret to learn that you still require sight L/C[3].   As you know, from the moment we open an L/C[4], our funds[5] will be tied up[6] for as long as 5 months, which is indeed a burden for the business development of any company.   We've been placing regular orders with you for years and our past dealings were always pleasant and satisfactory to both of us. So this time I'd like to propose a different way of payment, namely[7], T/T against[8] copy of B/L[9].   Hope this is agreeable[10] to you. We will send you the order upon receipt of your confirmation.   Best regards,   Grant

Task：

Write a reply to the above e-mail based on the following situation：

You have been dealing with this customer for five years, during which no problem has ever occurred. And as you have learned, this customer is of sound financial standing and good reputation.

Brainstorming：

What are the advantages and drawbacks of L/C payment for both the sellers and the buyers in international trade?

NOTES：

1. T/T：电汇，全称是 telegraphic transfer
国际贸易中常用的付款方式（terms of payment）有：
Remittance 汇付，包括：
（1）M/T（Mail Transfer）信汇
（2）T/T（Telegraphic Transfer）电汇
（3）D/D（Demand Draft）票汇
L/C（Letter of Credit）信用证
Collection 托收，包括：
（1）D/P（Documents against Payment）付款交单
（2）D/A（Documents against Acceptance）承兑交单
国际贸易中常用的付款工具（instruments of payment）有：
draft, bill of exchange 汇票
check/cheque 支票
promissory note 本票

2. terms of payment/payment terms：支付方式，付款条件
payment n. 支付，付款
payment in advance 预付
payment by installments 分期付款
payment on arrival of goods 货到付款

3. sight L/C：即期信用证
也可以表述为：
L/C at sight
L/C payable/available by draft at sight
远期信用证：usance/time/term L/C
远期信用证按起算日期不同分为：

L/C payable by draft at 30 days after sight 见票后 30 天付款的远期信用证

L/C payable by draft at 30 days after B/L date 提单日后 30 天付款的远期信用证

L/C payable by draft at 30 days after invoice date 发票日后 30 天付款的远期信用证

4. open an L/C：开立信用证

也可以表述为：

establish an L/C

issue an L/C（从银行角度）

5. funds：*n.*（复数形式）资金，现款

6. tie up：占压（资金）

All my money is tied up in property.

我所有的资金都投在房地产上了，无法动用。

7. namely：*adv.* 即，就是

8. against：*prep.* 凭，根据

D/P：documents against payment 付款交单

类似表达：under   *prep.* 在……（类别、书目、文书等）项下的

The goods under our S/C No. TY09 have been loaded onto S. S. Sweet.

我方 TY09 号销售合同项下的货物已装到 Sweet 号轮上。

9. copy of B/L：提单副本

10. agreeable：*adj.* 合意的

Part 2 | Learning about a similar task

Sample e-mail 1：Inquiring about terms of payment

From：bob. miller@ dimed. es
To：david_wen@ blues. com
Date：June 8, 20—
Subject：Your payment terms?
Dear Mr. Wen, Thank you for your samples. After a close study, we are glad to tell you that we find much interest in most of them, and have confidence that your goods will find a ready market at this end[1]. But there is still one thing left not discussed. Would you please state the payment terms you usually accept for your exports?

We look forward to your prompt reply.

Best regards,
Bob Miller

NOTES：

1. at this end：在此地，在我地
at our end 在我地
at your end 在你地

Sample e-mail 2：A Reply to the above

From：david. wen@ blues. com
To：bob_miller@ dimed. es
Date：June 8，20--
Subject：RE：Your payment terms?
Dear Mr. Miller, We really appreciate your intention to push the sales of our products in your country. Thank you very much. In reply, we'd like to inform you that we generally accept payment by T/T, i. e. , 30% deposit[1] after order confirmation but before mass production[2], and the balance[3] against copy of B/L. We hope the terms will be acceptable to you and wish to enter into[4] business with you soon. Best regards, David Wen

NOTES：

1. deposit：*n.* 订金
2. mass production：大批量生产，大货生产
3. balance：*n.* 余额
balance：*n.* 余额；差额
trade balance：贸易差额

the balance 70% = the rest 70% = the remaining 70%：70% 的余款部分

4. enter into：开始，达成，建立

to enter into an agreement 达成协议

to enter into business relations 建立业务关系

They refuse to enter into any discussion on this matter.

他们拒绝就此事进行任何探讨。

Brainstorming：

What are the strengths and weaknesses of T/T payment, compared with L/C?

Sample e-mail 3：Request for easier terms of payment

From：ben. clark@ ysh. com
To：richard-wang@ eipp. com. cn
Date：Sept. 25, 20—
Subject：terms of payment
Dear Richard,   As to payment terms, we wonder if you could grant us T/T terms. As one of the leading importers of chemicals[1] in Manila, Philippines, we have had no difficulties in meeting our obligations[2] and have always settled our account promptly[3]. If you need references[4], we will be glad to supply them to you.   We look forward to your confirmation of our first order, and hope it will mark the beginning of our pleasant business relations in the future.   Best regards,   Ben Clark

NOTES：

1. chemical：*n.* 化工品

2. meet our obligations：如期偿还债务

meet：*v.* 满足，达到，完成；支付

They will only agree to sign the contract if certain conditions are met.

只有某些条件得到了满足，他们才会同意签合同。

The company has agreed to meet all our expenses.

公司已同意支付我们所有的费用。

We believe you will meet our draft on presentation.

我们相信你方在汇票提交时付款。

obligation：*n.* 义务，债务

3. settle our account promptly：迅速结账

settle：*v.* 解决；结算

You are requested to settle your account quarterly.

请按季度结账。

It took the insurance company months to settle my claim.

保险公司用了好几个月才付清我的理赔金。

4. reference：*n.* （资信）证明书；备询人，资信征询公司

Banker's Reference 银行资信证明书

reference bank 备询银行，参考银行

Sample e-mail 4：Request rejected[1]

From：richard-wang@ eipp. com. cn
To：ben. clark@ ysfh. com
Date：Sept. 26, 20—
Subject：Re：terms of payment
Dear Ben， We have considered your request for payment by T/T and regret that we can't grant[2] the terms you asked for. We hope you will understand that the urgency of your order left us with insufficient[3] time to make the usual status inquiries[4] and we therefore have no choice but to follow our usual practice[5] with new customers, i. e. payment by sight L/C[6]. Maybe after several smooth and satisfactory transactions, we can consider other easier terms. We look forward to your confirmation and regular dealings. Best regards， Richard Wang

NOTES：

1. reject：*v.* 拒绝

The prime minister rejected the suggestion that it was time for him to resign.

首相拒绝了他该辞职的建议。

2. grant：*v.* 给予，同意

They granted her an entry visa.

他们发给她入境签证。

She granted their request.

她答应了他们的请求。

3. insufficient：*adj.* 不够的，不足的

4. status inquiry：资信询查

status：*n.* 情况，状态

credit status 信用状况

financial status 资金状况

credit and financial status 资信状况

5. We have no choice but to follow our usual practice.

我们只得按我方惯例办。

have no choice but to . . . ：除……外别无他法，不得不……

As our stocks are running low, we regret we have no choice but to decline your order.

由于我们的存货正在减少，我们不得不谢绝你方订货。

follow：*v.* 按照执行

We hope you will strictly follow our shipping instructions.

希望你方严格按照我们的装运要求办理。

6. payment by sight L/C：以即期信用证方式支付

by 表示支付的方式，如：

to pay by collection 用托收方式支付

payment by check 用支票支付

in 表示支付的货币，如：

to pay in Canadian dollar 用加元支付

payment in euro 用欧元支付

We usually pay by T/T or D/P.

我们通常用电汇或付款交单方式支付。

Do you accept payment in Renminbi?

你们接受人民币付款吗？

Brainstorming：

Suppose you were a seller, what payment terms would you adopt for a deal with a new customer in your export business? Please tick the appropriate box(es).

☐ sight L/C

□ T/T, 30% deposit, 70% against copy of B/L

□ T/T on arrival

Sample e-mail 5：Payment terms for an order with an E-shop

From：petersonsun@163.com
To：antonio8765@gmail.com
Date：Dec. 15, 20--
Subject：Re：terms of payment
Dear Antonio,   Thank you for your e-mail inquiring about the payment terms we require.   We usually accept Visa Card, MasterCard, Debit Card[1] and T/T for online orders and L/C, T/T and Western Union for offline orders.   f there is a price adjustment[2], please order the items first and make the payment after we revise the price.   We will send you e-mails to let you know your payment has been received and when your order has been shipped.   If you are still unclear about the payment procedures, please e-mail us.   Thank you very much for your support to our store.   Best wishes,   Peterson

NOTES：

1. debit card：借记卡
2. price adjustment：价格调整

Useful expressions

Payment by L/C 信用证支付
As you know, when applying for the issuance/establishment/opening of L/C, we have to pay a deposit in the bank. It has really cost us a great deal.   如你所知，在申请开证时，我们必须在银行交押金。这使我们花费很大。

For transactions involving an amount exceeding USD100,000, we always require sight L/C, which is our policy. Therefore we regret being unable to accept your D/P terms.
对于超过 10 万美元的交易，我们一贯要求即期信用证，这是我们公司的政策。因此，非常遗憾不能接受你方付款交单的方式。

Provided you fulfill the L/C terms, we will accept the drafts drawn under the L/C.
如果您履行信用证条款，我们即承兑依据此信用证所开的汇票。

We should be grateful if you could grant the credit asked for.
如能同意我们所要求的信用证支付方式，我们将非常感激。

Payment by T/T 电汇支付

We believe we have proved trustworthy business partners to each other after these years of satisfactory cooperation. So we should think that we deserve some easier terms of payment, say, T/T against copy of shipping documents.
我们相信经过这么多年的令人满意的合作，我们互相之间已经证明是值得信赖的合作伙伴。因此我们认为我们应得到更宽松一些的支付方式，如，凭装船单据副本电汇。

With a view to encouraging future business, we are pleased to accept your proposal for payment by T/T for future deals.
为了鼓励将来的业务，我们非常高兴地接受你方对于将来的交易采用电汇支付的建议。

As usual, our terms of payment are still by T/T, 40% in advance, and 60% paid within one week after B/L copy.
和往常一样，我们的支付方式仍然是电汇，预付 40%，收到提单副本后一周内支付 60%。

If it's acceptable, I will wire you USD150 for the expenses of the samples.
如果您接受的话，我将电汇 150 美元以支付样品的费用。

We've made you a remittance of CAD3,000 for payment of the 20% of freight due.
我们已汇付 3000 加元以支付所欠的 20% 运费。

We can only pay 20% in advance and the balance will be remitted when the goods are shipped.
我们只能预付 20%，余额在货物装运后汇付。

Payment by D/P or D/A 付款交单/承兑交单支付

As agreed, the terms of payment for the above order are D/P sight draft or 30 days D/A.
按照双方商定，上述订单的支付方式是即期付款交单或 30 天期承兑交单。

For this particular order, we agree to your suggestion of D/P payment so as to facilitate your sales of this product.
对这笔交易，我们同意你方 D/P 付款的建议，以利你方推销产品。

We have accepted your bill and we now have the documents. We shall collect the consignment as soon as it arrives in Bonn and honor your draft at maturity.
我方已承兑你方汇票并拿到单据。货物一到波恩我们立即提货并将在汇票到期时予以支付。

Payment by PayPal, Western Union or credit card etc. 贝宝、西联、信用卡等支付

As the amount involved is small, we suggest payment by credit card, PayPal or Western Union.

由于所涉金额少，我们建议采用信用卡、贝宝或西联支付。

I'd like to pay by PayPal to cover the samples as it's more convenient. Please give me your account number.

样品的费用，我想用贝宝支付，因为其更方便一些。请提供您的账户。

On AliExpress, all major credit cards and bank cards are accepted through the secure payment processor ESCROW.

通过安全支付处理系统——国际支付宝，速卖通平台可接受主要的信用卡和银行卡付款。

Please also make sure that you have used a Visa or MasterCard personal credit card to make the payment.

请确保使用 Visa 或是 MasterCard 个人信用卡来完成支付。

Follow the steps below to pay your order on AliExpress.

按照以下步骤完成速卖通订单支付。

Before you bid or buy, check the listing to see which payment methods the seller accepts.

在你出价或者购买前，请查看列表了解卖家所接受的付款方式。

Part 3　Getting prepared for your task

Ⅰ. Pattern drills. Make sentences with the following italicized expressions.

1. *Would you please state* the payment terms you usually accept for your exports?

A. 请说明贵方通常采用的包装方法。

B. 请说明你们的最早交货期。

C. 请说明此款式适用的面料成分。

D. 请说明此信用证的有效期(validity)。

2. *We'd like to inform you that* we generally accept payment by T/T.

A. 我们想告知你方我们通常采用的支付方式是电汇30%订金，余额凭提单副本支付。

B. 我们想告知你方由于第一笔交易，我们要求50%订金。

C. 我们想告知你方由于金额较大，我们要求采用信用证支付。

D. 我们想告知你方我们与新客户的惯例是即期信用证。

3. *We therefore have no choice but to* follow our usual practice with new customers.

A. 因此我们不得不建议采用电汇支付方式。

B. 因此我们不得不要求你方提供银行资信证明。

C. 因此我们不得不坚持我们的原价。

D. 采用信用证支付，资金占压时间过长，因此我们不得不要求更改支付方式。

II. Translate the following phrases into Chinese.

L/C at sight	T/T against copy B/L
D/P	Visa Credit Card
PayPal	MasterCard Credit Card
ESCROW	debit card
Western Union	deposit

III. Fill in the blanks with the right word or words and then put them into Chinese.

1. We have _____ (entered into, entered) a provisional agreement on the technological transfer.

2. When you make the offer, would you please _____ (inform, state) the earliest time of shipment?

3. We need an agent in that country to help us to _____ (push the sale of, push sale with) our products.

4. We appreciate the _____ (confidence, confidential) you have placed in us in the past and look forward to further dealings with you.

5. Should the Christmas Bear be of _____ (interest, interesting) to you, please let us know.

6. We have considered your request for T/T _____ (payment, pay) and accept it for this order.

7. Our brand of silk shirts has entered the market and we are sure that they will _____ (find a good market, find good market) _____ (in your end, at your end).

8. The end-users have no _____ (intention, interest) of importing the machines.

9. We refer to our L/C No. 305 covering 2,000 m/t steel shipped on 3rd October. The shipping documents were _____ (presented, present) to us yesterday.

10. Our usual terms of payment are 30% deposit by T/T before production and the _____ _____ (balance, balancing) against copy of B/L, or by L/C at sight.

IV. Fill in each of the following blanks with a word chosen from the list given.

order	grant	suppliers	satisfactory	by L/C
terms	favorable	time	on T/T basis	

Dear Ms. Wen,

We are pleased to learn from your e-mail that you have been able to ship our _____ in good _____ but we are surprised that you still demand payment _____.

After many years of _____ trading we feel that we are entitled to more _____ terms. Most of our _____ are doing business with us _____ and we should be grateful if you could _____ us the same _____.

We are looking forward to your favorable reply.

Best regards,
Willa White

Part 4 Getting your task done

Now please write an e-mail based on your task in Part 1.

Part 5 Broadening your knowledge

不同的跨境收款方式差别很大，有着不同的金额限制和到账速度，而且各自都有优缺点和适用范围。

一、线上跨境支付方式

1. Credit card 信用卡

（1）优点

信用卡是欧美最流行的支付方式，信用卡用户群非常庞大。

（2）缺点

接入方式较麻烦，且需预存保证金。信用卡收款费用高，而且黑卡很多，存在拒付风险。

（3）适用范围

很多跨境电商平台都支持国际信用卡支付。目前国际上有五大信用卡品牌：Visa、MasterCard、AmericaExpress、JCB、Diners Club，其中前两个使用较广泛。

2. PayPal 贝宝

（1）收款方费用

无开户费及使用费；每笔收取 0.3 美元的银行系统占用费；跨境交易，每笔收取 0.5% 的跨境费；每笔提现收取 35 美元。

（2）优点

PayPal 与支付宝较类似，是美国 eBay 旗下的支付平台，在国际上知名度较高，是很多国家客户的常用付款方式。

（3）缺点

每笔交易除手续费外还需要支付交易处理费。交易费用主要由商户提供。而且账户容易被冻结。

（4）适用范围：

适合跨境电商零售行业，几十到几百美元的小额交易。

3. Cashpay

（1）收款方费率：2.5%

（2）优点：可选择提现币种；加快偿付速度（2～3 天），结算快；安全性高，有专门的风险控制防欺诈系统。

（3）缺点：刚进入中国市场，国内知名度不高。

4. Moneybookers

（1）费用

免手续费，提现会收取少量费用。

（2）优点

安全，以 e-mail 为支付标识，不需要暴露信用卡等个人信息，只需要电子邮箱。

（3）缺点

不允许多账户，一个客户只能注册一个账户。

目前不支持未成年人注册，需年满 18 岁才可以。

5. Payoneer

Payoneer 是一家总部位于纽约的在线支付公司，主要业务是帮助其合作伙伴，将资金下发到全球，其同时也为全球客户提供美国银行/欧洲银行收款账户，用于接收欧美电商平台和企业的贸易款项。

（1）优点

中国身份证即可完成 Payoneer 账户在线注册，并自动绑定美国银行账户和欧洲银行账户。可以像欧美企业一样接收欧美公司的汇款，并通过 Payoneer 和中国支付公司的合作，完成线上的外汇申报和结汇。而且费用不高，笔单不超过 2%。

（2）适用人群

单笔资金额度小但是客户群分布广的跨境电商网站或卖家。

6. ClickandBuy

ClickandBuy 是独立的第三方支付公司。收到 ClickandBuy 的汇款确认后，在 3 ~ 4 个工作日内会收到货款。每次交易金额最低 100 美元，每天最高交易金额 $10,000。

7. PaysafeCard

PaysafeCard 购买手续简单而安全。除线上支付外，它还是欧洲游戏玩家的网游支付手段。用户用 16 位账户数字完成付款。

8. WebMoney

WebMoney 是俄罗斯最主流的电子支付方式，俄罗斯各大银行均可自主充值取款。

9. CashU

隶属于阿拉伯门户网站 Maktoob（Yahoo 于 2009 年完成对 Maktoob 的收购）。主要用于支付在线游戏、电信和 IT 服务，以及实现外汇交易。CashU 允许使用任何货币进行支付，但该帐户将始终以美元显示资金。CashU 现已为中东和独联体广大网民所使用，是中东和北非地区运用最广泛的电子支付方式之一。

10. LiqPAY

LiqPAY 是一个小额支付系统。一次性付款不超过 2500 美元，且立即到账，无交易次数限制。LiqPAY 用客户的移动电话号码为标识。账户存款是美元，所以如果你存另一种货币，将根据 LiqPAY 内部汇率折算。

11. QiwiWallet

QiwiWallet 是俄罗斯最大的第三方支付工具，其服务类似于支付宝。该系统使客户能够快速，方便的在线支付水电费、手机话费以及网购费用。还能用来偿付银行贷款。

二、线下跨境支付方式

1. T/T 电汇

（1）费用

买卖双方各自承担所在地的银行费用。具体费用根据银行的实际费率计算。

（2）优点

收款迅速，几分钟到账。先付款后发货，保证商家利益不受损失。

（3）缺点

先付款后发货，买方容易产生不信任。买卖双方都要支付手续费，而且费用较高。

（4）适用范围

电汇是传统 B2B 付款常用模式，适合大额的交易付款。

2. Western Union 西联汇款

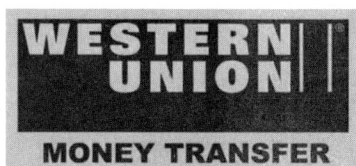

西联汇款是世界上领先的特快汇款方式，可以在全球大多数国家汇出和提款。

（1）费用

西联手续费由买家承担。需要买卖双方到当地银行实地操作。在卖家未收款时，买家随时可以撤销资金。

（2）优点

到账速度快；手续费由买家承担，对于卖家来说很划算；可先提钱再发货，安全性好。

（3）缺点

由于对买家来说风险极高，买家不易接受。买家和卖家需要去西联线下柜台操作。

手续费较高。

（4）适用范围

1 万美元以下的中等额度支付。

3. MoneyGram 速汇金

MoneyGram，又称速汇金汇款。在全球 150 个国家和地区，拥有总数超过 50,000 个的代理网点。收款人凭汇款人提供的编号即可收款。国内目前有工行、交行、中信银行三家代理了速汇金收付款服务。

（1）优势

汇款速度快，十几分钟即可账；汇款金额不高时，费用相对较低，无中间行费，无电报费；手续简单，无须填写复杂的汇款路径，收款人无须预先开立银行账户。

（2）缺点：

汇款人及收款人均必须为个人；必须为境外汇款；客户如持现钞账户汇款，还需交纳一定的现钞变汇的手续费。

4. L/C 信用证

信用证，指的是开证行应申请人要求和指示，向第三方开立的载有一定金额的，在一定期限内符合规定的单据付款的书面保证文件。

（1）优点

信用证是国际贸易中最复杂的付款方式，也是安全系数相对较高的一种。

（2）缺点

手续复杂烦琐。因为里面至少涉及四个角色：信用证申请人、开证行、通知行、信用证受益人。

不符点。虽然理论上不符点可以避免，但是现实操作中，几乎很难碰到完完全全无任何不符点的信用证议付。单据和信用证规定的任何差异都可以称为不符点，比如一个字母或者一个标点，银行都有理由以此为不符点并扣款。

5. D/P & D/A 付款交单和承兑交单

D/P，付款交单，指卖方将出货后的相关单据提交给银行，买方通过当地托收行付款赎单，然后提货。

D/A，承兑交单，指卖方在货物装运后出具汇票，连同各种单据通过银行指示买方，而买方在汇票上办理承兑后，就可以凭单据提货。

虽然 D/P 和 D/A 的操作比信用证简便许多，费用上也少了一个通知行的费用，但是银行在托收过程中是不承担任何风险和责任的。

Task 10   Covering More Risks

LEARNING OBJECTIVES:

☞ To be able to write e-mails negotiating the insurance coverage, amount, premium etc.

☞ To get familiar with the writing plans, useful sentences and phrases of negotiating insurance terms

Part 1   Getting to know your task

Scenario:

Risks in cargo transportation are of many kinds. Different risks mean different losses. Here is a news event. While a Chinese exporter and a European importer are now negotiating details of E-contract intended, they both learn the news that in the destination port, Algeciras[1], strikes[2] are going from March, 2017. Port cargo backlog[3] will certainly affect the delivery time[4].

Task:

Write an e-mail to clarify the insurance clauses with the European company.

Brainstorming:

What additional insurance should be included in this e-mail?

NOTES:

1. Algeciras: 阿尔赫西拉斯(西班牙南部港口城市)
2. strike: *v. n.* 罢工
3. port cargo backlog: 港口货物积压
4. delivery time: 交货时间
5. APM Terminals: 马士基集装箱码头公司 APM 指的是 A. P. Moller-Maersk，马士基集团，马士基集装箱码头公司是该集团下的子公司。该集团旗下另一家著名的子公

司——马士基航运公司(Maersk Line)，为世界上最大的集装箱航运公司

6. The International Dockworkers' Council：简称 IDC，国际码头工人委员会

7. bill：法案

APM Terminals[5] is present in Algeciras, Spain's biggest port.
Photo: APM Terminals

Port strikes could go global on Friday

PORTS: The International Dockworkers' Council[6] is planning coordinated strikes in Europe and the rest of the world on Friday to signal solidarity with the Spanish port workers, which are currently in a conflict with the government concerning a new bill[7].

Part 2　Learning about a similar task

Sample e-mail 1：Covering insurance on CIF basis

From：Tonyzhang@ cherry. com
To：blackberrysmith@ terseed. com
Subject：insurance
Attachment：Quotation. pdf
Dear Mr. Smith,

Attached is our CIF quotation for Hand Tools and we are sure you will find our prices workable[1]. Regarding[2] insurance[3], please note the following：

—— We usually insure[4] the goods sold on CIF basis with our underwriter[5], the People's Insurance Company of China (PICC) for 110% of total invoice value against All Risks[6] as per the Ocean Marine Cargo Clauses of PICC of January 1, 1981[7]. ——If a higher percentage or broader coverage[8] is required, the extra premium[9] will be for the buyer's account[10].

As to PICC, we wish to inform you that PICC is a state-owned company with agents in practically all the major cities and seaports in the world. It is renowned for[11] settling claims promptly and equitably. As far as we know, the rates they quote are among the most competitive in the industry. If you have further questions, please let us know.

We look forward to receiving orders from you.

Best regards,
Tony Zhang

NOTES:

1. workable：*adj.* 切实可行的，可使用的
They held this way to be workable.
他们认为这个方法是可行的。

2. regarding：prep. 关于，至于
Regarding payment, we would like to pay by an irrevocable sight Letter of Credit.
至于付款，我们想以不可撤销的即期信用证付款。
Please let us have all necessary information regarding your products for export.
请告知所有关于你们出口产品的必要信息。
还可以表述为：in regard to, with regard to, as regards
We have already written to you in regard to this matter.
关于此事，我们已写信给你了。
With regard to your e-mail of May 6, we regret we cannot comply with your wishes.
关于你方5月6日的来信，很遗憾我们不能满足你的要求。
As regards the balance, we will advise you of the position in a few days.
关于余数，将于日内告知。

3. insurance：*n.* 保险
insurance amount 保险金额，保值　　insurance premium 保险费，保险费率
insurance policy 保险单　　　　　　insurance certificate 保险凭证
insurance company 保险公司　　　　insurance coverage 保险范围
insurance clause 保险条款
"投保"的动宾搭配通常有：
cover/effect/arrange/take out insurance 投保，办理保险
effect insurance 投保
insurance 一词有下列介词可以搭配：

insurance on 保险的标的物

insurance on 1,000 sets electric fans 为 1000 台电风扇投保

insurance for 保险金额

insurance for 110% of the invoice value 按发票金额的 110% 投保

insurance against 保险险别

insurance against All Risks and War Risk 投保一切险和战争险

insurance at 保险费

insurance at a premium of 5‰ 按 5‰的保险费投保

insurance with 保险公司

insurance with PICC 在中国人民保险公司投保

We have covered insurance on your order with PICC for 110% of the invoice value against All Risks and War Risk.

我们已在中国人民保险公司对你们的订货按发票金额的 110% 投保了一切险和战争险。

4. insure：*v.* 保险

insure 一词有下列介词可以搭配：

insure 后直接跟保险的标的物，不加介词

insure 1,000 sets of electric fans 为 1000 台电风扇投保

insure us 为我们人身投保

insure for 保险金额

insure for 110% of the invoice value 按发票金额的 110% 投保

insure against 保险险别

insure against All Risks and War Risk 投保一切险和战争险

insure at 保险费

insure at a premium of 5‰按 5‰的保险费投保

insure with 保险公司

insure with PICC 在中国人民保险公司投保

We normally insure this item against All Risks and TPND.

这种货我们通常投保一切险和偷窃、提货不着险。

This insurance policy insures us against All Risks.

本保险单为我们投保了一切险。

We usually insure for 10% above the invoice value.

我们通常按发票金额的 110% 投保。

Do you insure against FWRD on this item?

这种货你们投保淡水雨淋险吗？

5. underwriter：*n.* 保险公司；保险业者

6. All Risks 一切险

All Risks：一切险，按照中国人民保险公司 1981 年 1 月 1 日修订的《海洋运输货物

保险条款》规定，海洋运输保险的基本险别分为：

平安险（Free from Particular Average，F. P. A. ）

水渍险（With Particular Average 或 With Average ，W. P. A. 或 W. A. ）

一切险（All Risks，A. R. ）

7. Ocean Marine Cargo Clauses of PICC of January 1，1981：中国人民保险公司（PICC）1981 年 1 月 1 日修订的《海洋运输货物保险条款》

8. coverage：*n.* 保险；承保险别；保险范围（包括险别、保值、保险起止地等）

What types of coverage do you usually underwrite?

你们公司通常承保什么险？

If the business is concluded on CIF terms, what coverage will you take out?

如果以 CIF 价成交，你们将投保什么险？

9. premium：*n.* 保险费

extra premium = additional premium 额外保费

10. for the buyer's account：记在……的账上；由……负担

This can be done provided that the cost, air freight and insurance premium are for the buyer's account.

成本、航邮费及保险费须由买方客户负担。

The demurrage is for account of the exporter.

滞期费由出口商支付。

"由……支付/负担"的常用表达方式还有：

at one's cost/expense

to be borne by sb.

to be charged to one's account

Freight for shipment from Shanghai to Hong Kong is to be charged to your account.

从上海到香港的运费由贵方负担。

11. be renowned for：因……而著名

Sample e-mail 2：Covering additional risks

From：peterli@ 126. com
To：lila. bright@ yatex. com
Date：Nov 18，20--
Subject：covering an additional risk
Dear Lila, We would like to inform you of insurance as follows：

Generally we cover[1] WPA for 110% of the invoice value with PICC in the absence of[2] definite[3] instructions from our clients. If you desire to cover All Risks, we can provide such coverage at a slightly higher premium.

Additionally, for cargos that are highly fragile and valuable, we usually recommend our clients to cover Breakage[4], a special risk in your interest, for which an extra premium will have to be charged[5]. The present rate[6] is about 3‰.

We await your early reply.

Best regards,
Peter Li

NOTES

1. cover: *v.* 保险，投保

We wish to cover the goods against All Risks.

我们想投保一切险。

You're requested to cover War Risk in addition to All Risks.

除一切险外，请加保战争险。

Insurance is to be covered by the buyers.

由买方办理保险。

This insurance policy has covered us against All Risks and War Risk.

这份保单给我们保了一切险和战争险。

We usually cover 110% of the invoice value.

我们通常投保发票金额的110%。

cover: *n.* 保险 = insurance cover

Does your policy provide adequate cover against Breakage?

你们的保单提供足够的破碎险吗?

2. in the absence of: 没有，在没有……的情况下

We cannot ship the goods in the absence of your L/C.

没有你方信用证，我们不能装运此货。

3. definite: adj. 明确的，确切的

4. Breakage: *n.* 破碎险，一般附加险的一种

根据海洋货物运输保险条款(OMCC，即 Ocean Marine Cargo Clause)，中国人民保险公司承保的附加险有一般附加险和特殊附加险两种。

一般附加险：(General Additional Risks)

Theft, Pilferage and Non-delivery (T. P. N. D.) 偷窃提货不着险

Fresh Water and/or Rain Damage（FWRD）淡水雨淋险

Shortage 短量险   Intermixture and Contamination 混杂沾污险

Leakage 渗漏险   Clash and Breakage 碰损破碎险

Taint of Odour 串味险   Sweat and Heating 受潮受热险

Hook Damage 钩损险   Breakage of Packing 包装破碎险

Rust 锈损险

特殊附加险：（Special Additional Risks）

War Risk 战争险   Strikes 罢工险

Aflatoxin 黄曲霉素险   Failure to Deliver 交货不到险

On Deck 舱面险   Import Duty 进口关税险

Rejection 拒收险

5. charge：v. 收取费用；记账

We charge them RMB5,000 for storage.

我们向他们收取存储费5000元。

Shall we charge the flowers to your account?

我们可以把这些花记到你的账上吗?

charge n. 费用

There is an additional charge for sending shipments by air.

空运货物要追加费用。

If the material is found faulty, we will replace it free of charge.

如果发现材料有缺点，我们将免费更换。

6. rate：n. = insurance premium rate(保险)费率

rate 还有"价格"的意思

What's the going rate for this type of machine tool?

这种机床的现价是多少?

Brainstorming：

What special additional risks can we cover the goods against? Please tick the appropriate box(es).

☐ All Risks.

☐ Breakage

☐ Strikes

☐ War Risk

Useful expressions

Insurance arrangement 投保
Insurance is to be covered by the buyer under FOB terms. 按照 FOB 条件下由买方投保。 Please insure us on the following goods. 请为我方投保下列货物。 We shall arrange insurance on your behalf. 我方将代你方办理投保手续。

Insurance coverage 保险范围
Please take out cover on all our purchases of leathers against TPND, Contamination, Fresh and/or Rain Water Damage in addition to WPA. 在投保水渍险的同时，请为这批购买的皮革投保偷窃提货不着险、沾污险和淡水雨淋险等附加险。 Insurance is to be covered against WPA and against War Risk in the absence of definite instructions from our clients. 在客户没有明确指定险种的情况下，我方投保水渍险和战争险。 The buyer said that he would cover insurance against All Risks on the goods. 买方说他会为货物投保一切险。

Insurance Amount 保险金额
We usually insure against All Risks for 110% of the invoice value. 我们通常按照发票金额的110%投保一切险。 We usually insure against All Risks for 10% above the invoice value. 我们通常按照发票金额的110%投保一切险。 We usually insure against All Risks for the invoice value plus 10%. 我们通常按照发票金额的110%投保一切险。 Although it is our usual practice to insure shipments for the invoice value plus 10%, we are prepared to comply with you request for getting cover for 130% of the invoice value with the extra premium for your account. 虽然我们通常的做法是为货物投保发票金额加成10%，但这次我们愿意应你方要求，按发票金额的130%计算投保金额，额外保费将由你方支付。

The insurer 保险人
We usually have our exports insured with the People's Insurance Company of China. 我们通常在中国人民保险公司为我们的出口货物投保。 Insurance is to be effected by the sellers against All Risks for 110% of the invoice value with the People's Insurance Company of China. 由卖方按发票金额110%向中国人民保险公司投保一切险。

Part 3 **Getting prepared for your task** ▶ ▶ ▶

Ⅰ. Pattern drills. Make sentences with the following italicized expressions.

1. We usually *insure against* All Risks for 110% of the invoice value.

A. 我们已按发票金额的 110% 投保了水渍险及战争险。

B. 你方可以按发票金额的 130% 为该货投保这些险吗?

C. 请按发票金额的 110% 投保破碎险(Breakage)。

D. 每家公司都给自己的财产(property)保险,以防发生损失。

2. We have *covered insurance on* 1,000 sets of refrigerators *for* 130% of the invoice value *against* All Risks *with* PICC.

A. 我们已向中国人民保险公司为 2000 台彩色电视机按发票金额的 110% 投保一切险。

B. 我们已向中国人民保险公司为 3000 箱皮鞋按发票金额的 110% 投保水渍险。

C. 我们已向中国人民保险公司为 5000 箱龙井茶按发票金额的 120% 投保平安险。

D. 我们已向中国人民保险公司为 100 公吨羊毛按发票金额的 130% 投保一切险。

3. Extra premium is *for the buyer's account* should additional risks be covered.

A. 应你方要求已代为标题货物向中国人民保险公司投保一切险,保额 3200 英镑,保费由你方支付。

B. 破碎险属于一般附加险,我方可以为你方加保破碎险,但保险费由你方支付。

C. 我们还可以安排投保一切险及战争险以外的险别,但额外保费也应由买方支付。

D. 由于合同规定按发票金额的 110% 投保,如你方要求按 130% 投保,额外保费应由你方支付。

Ⅱ. Supply the missing words in the blanks.

terms	is	value	extra
risks	on	that	borne

Dear Mr. Bright,

Regarding the question of insurance, we wish to state _____ for transactions concluded on CIF _____, our usual practice _____ to cover All Risks and War Risk for 110% of the invoice _____. If you wish to cover other _____ that are under the Ocean Marine Cargo Clauses of the People's Insurance Company of China, we may do so _____ your behalf, but the _____ premium should be _____ by you.

Best regards,
Katy

Ⅲ. Correct the mistakes in the use of a preposition in the following sentences.

1. If you wish to cover the insurance to table-cloths against All Risks at 130% of the invoice value, you should be borne by the additional premium for the difference between 130% and 110%.

2. Please insure on the cargo against F. P. A. to our account.

3. We hope to receive the policy at 5,750 for our September shipment within the next few days.

4. The cargo sold on CIF basis shall be effected insurance by the buyers.

5. As contract No. 9927 stipulated, insurance is to be affected against 120% of the invoice value.

Ⅳ. Read the following insurance policy and then fill in the blanks based on the information given in this insurance policy.

1. The goods insured are ( ), which are shipped from ( ) to ( ).	
2. The name of the insured is ( ).	
3. The name of the insurer is ( ).	
4. The risks covered are ( ).	
5. The insurance amount is( ).	
6. The insurance premium is ( ).	
7. The insurance policy number is ( ).	

货物运输保险单
CARGO TRANSPORTATION INSURANCE POLICY

发票号(INVOICE NO.) IV0001972
合同号(CONTRACT NO.) contract02
信用证号(L/C NO.) 002/0000398

保单号次
POLICY NO. 1030001629

被保险人
Insured：RIQING EXPORT AND IMPORT COMPANY

本公司根据被保险人的要求, 由被保险人向本公司缴付约定的保险费, 按限本保险单保险别和背面所载条款与下列特殊承保下述货物运输保险, 特立本保险单。
THE COMPANY IN ACCORDANCE WITH THE REQUIREMENTS OF THE INSURED BY THE INSURED TO THE COMPANY AGREED TO PAY THE PREMIUMS, IN ACCORDANCE WITH THE INSURANCE COVERAGE AND ON THE BACK OF THE FOLLOWING TERMS AND CONDITIONS CONTAINED IN THE SPECIAL SECTION COVER THE CARRIAGE OF GOODS BY INSURANCE, OF THE INSURANCE TRINIDAD SINGLE

标记 MARKS&NOS	包装及数量 QUANTITY	保险货物项目 DESCRIPTION OF GOODS	保险金额 AMOUNT INSURED
CANNED LITCHIS JAPAN C/NO.1-1000 MADE IN CHINA	CARTONS	CANNED LITCHIS	JPY 1366855.00

总保险金额   壹佰叁拾陆万陆仟捌佰伍拾伍日元整
TOTAL AMOUNT INSURED:

保费   启运日期   装载运输工具
PREMIUM：JPY   10934.84   DATE OF COMMENCEMENT：2010-06-24   PER CONVEYANCE： TBA
目   经   至
FROM：SHANGHAI,CHINA   VIA：   TO：NAGOYA,JAPAN
承保险别
CONDITIONS：

COVERING ALL RISKS, OCEAN MARINE CARGO CLAUSES.

所保货物,如发生保险单项下可能引起索赔的损失或损坏,应立即通知本公司下述代理人查勘。如有索赔,应向本公司提交保单正本(本保险单共有3份正本)及有关文件。如一份正本已用于索赔, 其余正本自动失效。
IN THE EVENT OF LOSS OR DAMAGE WITCH MAY RESULT IN A CLAIM UNDER THIS POLICY, IMMEDIATE NOTICE MUST BE GIVEN TO THE COMPANY'S AGENT AS MENTIONED HEREUNDER. CLAIMS,IF ANY,ONE OF THE ORIGINAL POLICY WHICH HAS BEEN ISSUED IN 3 ORIGINAL(S) TOGETHER WITH THE RELEVENT DOCUMENTS SHALL BE SURRENDERED TO THE COMPANY . IF ONE OF THE ORIGINAL POLICY HAS BEEN ACCOMPLISHED. THE OTHERS TO BE VOID.

国际保险公司

INTERNATIONAL INSURANCE COMPANY

赔款偿付地点   JAPAN
CLAIM PAYABLE AT

出单日期   August 31th,2011
ISSUING DATE

Part 4   Getting your task done

Now please write an e-mail based on your task in Part 1.

Task 11　Making out Pro Forma Invoice and Sales Contract

LEARNING OBJECTIVES:

☞ To be able to write e-mails confirming a deal
☞ To be able to write e-mails confirming a deal

Part 1　Getting to know your task

Scenario:

The seller Alex Zhao, Sales Director in Qingdao Bright Artificial Plants Co., Ltd., and the buyer Robert Bach, Chairman of TJMAX HOMEWARE[1] have come to agreement on the essential terms and conditions of an order for silk flowers. Now Robert is sending an order as given below and asking for a pro forma invoice[2] from Alex.

From: robertbach@ tjmax. com
To: Alexzhao@ bright. com
Date: May 11, 20—
Subject: Order No. CL-MA80 for silk flowers
Dear Mr. Zhao, We have received your DHgate internal message[3] of May 10. After consideration, we have pleasure in placing an order[4] as follows: Product name: Artificial Silk Peony Flowers   Item Code: 259075753   Category: Decorative Flowers & Wreaths[5]   Color: Pink   Length: 50cm   Packaging: 55. 0 ×20. 0 ×30. 0 (cm)   Gross Weight: 0. 2kg   Quantity: 1,000 pieces

Quality：2017 new design
Price：US ＄7. 26/Piece
Payment：credit cards
Shipment：Free Shipping to United States Via ePacket，not later than May 17

Please send us your PROFORMA INVOICE for 1,000 pieces of silk flowers.

We hope this transaction[6] will mark a good beginning between us.

Yours sincerely，
Robert Bach

Task：

You are required as the seller to draft a return e-mail to confirm the order with a proforma invoice or a sales contract attached. The pro forma invoice form and sales contract form are in blank which you should fill in for the seller according to the order.

NOTES：

1. homeware：*n.* 家用产品
2. pro forma invoice：形式发票
常见发票种类还有：
Commercial Invoice 商业发票
Customs Invoice 海关发票
Consular Invoice 领事发票
3. GHgate internal message：敦煌网站内信
4. order：*n.* 订单
与 order 相关的短语有：
to execute/fulfill an order 执行订单
to accept/entertain an order 接受订单
to decline/refuse an order 拒绝订单
to complete/finish an order 完成订单
outstanding order 未交货订单
initial order 首个订单
trial order 试订单
repeat order 续订单，除交货期外，数量、价格等未必与原订单相同的订单
If the first order proves satisfactory，we will place with you many repeat orders.
如果首次订货令人满意，我们会大量续订。
duplicate order 除交货期外，其余条件同原订单完全一样的订单
As the cost has now advanced a lot，we regret we cannot accept your duplicate order at the

original level.

由于成本上涨了很多，抱歉不能按原来价格接受你们的重复订单。

5. decorative flowers & wreaths：装饰花和花环

6. transaction：*n.* 交易

We trust this transaction will prove to be a great success between us.

我方相信本次交易将会非常成功。

close/finalize/conclude a transaction 成交

We are pleased to close this transaction with you.

我们很高兴与你们达成这笔交易。

Brainstorming：

What is a Pro forma Invoice used for in international trade?

Part 2　Learning about a similar task

Sample e-mail 1：Buyers sending a purchase order[1]

From：Franz@ tse. com
To：Sissi@ rsm. com
Date：Sep 11，20—
Subject：Purchase Order No. CL-MA80 for female clothes

Dear Sissi，

Thank you so much for your message of 3rd Sep. and the catalogues. We find both the quality and prices satisfactory and are pleased to place our order No. CL-MA80 as follows：

Item	Item No.	Color	Unit Price USD CIF New York	Quantity	Subtotal[2]
Coat	CT23	Purple	120.00	100	12,000.00
		Brown	120.00	100	12,000.00
		Black	120.00	100	12,000.00
		Pink	125.00	100	12,500.00
Blouse	BS34	Blue print	16.00	200	3,200.00
Blouse	BS36	Red print	16.00	200	3,200.00
				Total 800	54,900.00

We expect to find a good market for the above and hope to place further and large orders with you in the near future[3]. Our usual terms of payment are credit cards and we hope they will be acceptable to you.

Please send us yoursales contract.

Best regards，

Franz

NOTES:

1. purchase order: 购货单, 客户订单, 简写为 P/O、P. O.
2. subtotal: *n.* 分项小计
3. in the near future: 在不久的未来

Brainstorming:

What details can we give in a purchase order? Please tick the appropriate box(es).

☐ Name of goods, catalogue and sample

☐ Price of goods, including unit price and total value

☐ Quality requirement, grade, model name/number and specifications

☐ Quantity of goods

☐ Origin and materials[1]

☐ Weight, dimensions, color and pattern

☐ Packaging and marking

☐ Terms of payment

☐ Delivery requirements[2], including place, date, mode of transport, whether the order will be carriage paid or carriage forward[3], etc.

☐ Documents such as bill of lading, commercial invoice and insurance policy

☐ Special points and others, for example, alternatives if goods required are not available

NOTES:

1. origin and materials: 原产地、材料
2. delivery requirement: 运输要求
3. carriage paid/carriage forward: 运费付讫/运费到付

Sample e-mail 2: Sellers sending a sales contract

From: Sissi@ rsm. com
To: Franz@ tse. com
Date: Sep 12, 20—
Subject: Re: Sales Contract[1] for P/O No. CL-MA80
Attachment: Sales Contract No. ZV109. pdf (1. 2M)
Dear Franz, We are pleased to receive your order CL-MA80 for female clothes. We accept the order and are sending you by attachment our Sales Contract No. ZV109 in duplicate[2] of which please countersign[3] and return one copy to us for our file[4]. We trust you will pay for the order by credit card at an early date.

We shall arrange delivery as soon as we receive your payment.

Hope the goods will prove to your entire satisfaction and we may have further orders from you.

Best regards,
Sissi

NOTES：

1. contract：*n.* 合同

Sales contract 销售合同，缩写为 S/C

Sales Confirmation 销售确认书，售货确认书，缩写为 S/C

contract：*v.* 订立合同；承包

We are pleased to contract with you for 1,000 Toy Pandas.

我们高兴地和你方订立 1000 只玩具熊猫的合同。

It is utterly important that shipment should be effected before the contracted deadline.

在合同规定的期限内完成装运是至关重要的。

Our company was contracted to build shelters for the homeless.

他们刚跟我们公司签订合同，为无家可归的人建造收容所。

The government contracted out hospital cleaning to private companies.

政府将医院的清洁工作承包给了私营公司。

2. in duplicate：一式两份

"一式……份"的说法有：

一式两份：in duplicate, in two copies, in two fold

一式三份：in triplicate, in three copies, in three fold

一式四份：in quadruplicate, in four copies, in four fold

duplicate：*n.* 一式两份中的任一份；副本

I lost the original form so they sent me a duplicate.

我丢失了表格正本，所以他们给我寄了一份副本。

duplicate：adj. 完全相同的

As the wool carpets enjoy fast sales in our market，we are glad to place a duplicate order with you.

由于羊毛地毯在我市场旺销，我们高兴地向你方重复订购。

duplicate：*v.* 重复，复制

As our clients are quite satisfied with your products，we will duplicate our last order.

因我方客户对你方产品相当满意，我们将按上次订单重复订购。

3. countersign：*v.* 会签，副署

Attached please find the duplicate contract countersigned by us.

兹附上我方会签的一份合同，请查收。

counter-signature：*n.* = countersignature 或 counter signature 会签，副署签名

Attached please find the duplicate contract with our countersignature.

兹附上我方会签的一份合同，请查收。

4. for our file：供我方存档

for one's record 供某人存档

The buyer is requested to sign and return one copy of this sales contract for the seller's file immediately after receipt of the same.

买方在收到销售合同后，应立即会签并退回一份供卖方存档。

相同结构的其他短语还有：

for one's reference   供某人参考

for one's information 供某人参考

for one's perusal 供某人详阅

for one's consideration 供某人考虑

ATTACHMENT

SALES CONTRACT（ORIGINAL）

Contract No.：ZV109 Date：Sep. 12，20——

Signed at：Nanjing，China

Sellers：ZEST Garments（Jiangsu）Import & Export Corporation

　　　　18 - 7 Dasifu Road，Qinhuai District，Nanjing，210000，China

Buyers：Pacific Trading Co.，Ltd

　　　　118 Green Road，New York，U. S. A.

This Sales Contract is made by and between the Sellers and the Buyers whereby the Sellers agree to sell and the Buyers agree to buy the under-mentioned goods according to the terms and conditions stipulated below：

1.

Name of Commodity	Color	Unit Price USD CIF New York	Quantity （pcs）	Subtotal
Coat Art. No. CT23	Purple	120. 00	100	12,000. 00
	Brown	120. 00	100	12,000. 00
	Black	120. 00	100	12,000. 00
	Pink	125. 00	100	12,500. 00
Blouse Art. No. BS34	Blue Print	16. 00	200	3,200. 00
Blouse Art. No. BS36	Red Print	16,00	200	3,200. 00
Total			800	54,900. 00

2. Packaging: One piece in a box, 10 boxes to a carton

3. Shipping Marks:

PTC

New York

No. 1–600

4. Time of Shipment: During November, 20—, allowing partial shipments and transshipment.

5. Port of Shipment: Shanghai, China

6. Port of Destination: New York, U. S. A.

7. The Sellers are allowed to load 5% more or less[1] and the price shall be calculated according to the unit price.

8. Insurance: To be covered by the Sellers for 110% of the invoice value against All Risks and War Risk as per the relevant Ocean Marine Cargo Clauses of the People's Insurance Company of China. If other coverage or an additional insurance amount is required, the Buyers must have the consent of the Sellers before shipment, and the additional premium is to be borne by the Buyers.

9. Terms of Payment: The Buyers shall open with a bank acceptable to the Sellers an irrevocable Letter of Credit at sight to reach the Sellers 30 days before the time of shipment specified, valid for negotiation in China until the 15th day after the aforesaid time of shipment.

10. Commodity Inspection: It is mutually agreed that the Certificate of Quality[2] issued by the State General Administration for Quality Supervision and Inspection and Quarantine[3] of P. R. China at the port of shipment shall be taken as the basis of delivery.

11. Discrepancy[4] and Claim: Any claim by the Buyers on the goods shipped shall be filed within 30 days after the arrival of the goods at the port of destination and supported by a survey report issued by a surveyor approved by the Sellers. Claims in respect to matters within the responsibility of the insurance company or of the shipping company will not be considered or entertained by the Sellers.

12. Force Majeure[5]: If shipment of the contracted goods is prevented or delayed in whole or in part due to Force Majeure, the Sellers shall not be liable for non-shipment or late shipment of the goods under this Contract. However, the Sellers shall notify the Buyers by fax or e-mail immediately and furnish a certificate issued by the China Council for the Promotion of International Trade attesting such event or events.

13. Arbitration[6]: All disputes arising out of the performance of or relating to this Contract shall be settled amicably through negotiation. In case no settlement can be reached through negotiation, the case shall then be submitted to the Foreign Economic and Trade Arbitration Commission[7] of the China Council for the Promotion of International Trade[8], Beijing, China, for arbitration in accordance with its Rules of Procedure. The award of the arbitration is final and binding upon both parties.

THE SELLERS

　　林新月

Chief Executive Officer

ZEST Garments（Jiangsu）

Import & Export Corporation

18－7 Dasifu Road，Qinhuai District

Nanjing，210000，China

THE BUYERS

Pacific Trading Co.，Ltd.

118 Green Road，New York，

U. S. A.

NOTES：

1. 5% more or less：5% 的溢短装

more or less clause 溢短装条款

Please insert the wording "5% more or less allowed" in the quantity clause.

请在数量条款中插入"允许溢短装 5%"的字句。

You are required to add "more or less clause" to the covering L/C.

我们要求你方在有关信用证中加上溢短装条款。

2. Certificate of Quality：质量检验证书

3. State General Administration for Quality Supervision and Inspection and Quarantine of P. R. China：简称为 AQSIQ，国家质量监督检验检疫总局

4. discrepancy：*n.* 不同，不符

There are some discrepancies in numbers.

在数字上有一些不符。

Such small discrepancies between the products and the sample are normal and permissible.

这种产品与样品之间的些微不同是在正常的允许范围之内。

5. Force Majeure：不可抗力，人力不可抗拒

In the event of Force Majeure, we shall not be held responsible for the late delivery or non-delivery of the goods.

如果发生不可抗力事件，我方将不为延期交货或未交货而承担责任。

6. arbitration：*n.* 仲裁

In case negotiation fails, the dispute should be submitted to arbitration.

如果协商不能解决，争议将被提交仲裁。

arbitration clause 仲裁条款

arbitration committee 仲裁委员会

voluntary arbitration 自愿仲裁

compulsory arbitration 强制仲裁

arbitrate：*v.* 仲裁

to arbitrate a dispute：仲裁一项争议

arbitrator：*n.* 仲裁人

arbitral：*adj.* 仲裁的

arbitral award 仲裁裁决

7. Foreign Economic and Trade Arbitration Commission：对外经济贸易仲裁委员会

8. China Council for the Promotion of International Trade（CCPIT）：中国国际贸易促进委员会

Sample E-mail 3：Sellers sending a pro forma invoice

From：Elizabeth@ nice. com
To：William@ Jan. com
Date：Sep. 6，20—
Subject：P/I No. PAP – 109 for P/O No. FT – 106
Attachment：P/I No. PAP – 109. pdf（1. 2M）
Dear William， Thank you for your P/O No. PAP – 109 and your efforts. We confirm having booked your order[1] for 1,000 pieces of Women's Cashmere Coats[2]. You may rest assured that our products are of excellent quality and exquisite workmanship[3]. We trust they will enjoy fast sales at your end. Attached is our P/I No. PAP – 109. Please sign it back[4]. Thank you in advance for your cooperation. Best regards， Elizabeth

NOTES：

1. book your order：接订，接受你方订货
We are pleased to book your order for 1,000 Mu Lan Brand Motorcycles.
我们高兴地接受你方 1000 辆木兰牌摩托车的订货。
book sth. with sb. = place an order with sb. for sth. 向某人订货
We have booked 10,000 cases of Sprite with the Coca – Cola Company for this event.
为这次活动，我们已经向可口可乐公司订购 1 万箱雪碧。
2. cashmere coat：羊绒大衣
3. exquisite workmanship：工艺精良，工艺也可以叫 craftsmanship
4. sign...back：签字并退回，会签

ATTACHMENT

<table>
<tr><td colspan="5" align="center">CAMELLIA GARMENTS CORPORATION
Room 2901, Shangri-La Mansion, 209 Donghai Road, Qingdao 266000, P. R. CHINA
TEL: 0532 – 88761006   FAX: 0532 – 88761007</td></tr>
<tr><td colspan="5" align="center">PRO FORMA INVOICE
TO: MAPLE TRADING CO. , LTD.   INVOICE NO. : PAP – 109</td></tr>
<tr><td colspan="3">129 QUEEN ST. , TORONTO, CANADA</td><td>INVOICE DATE:</td><td>SEP. 6, 20--</td></tr>
<tr><td>TERMS OF PAYMENT:</td><td colspan="4">BY T/T WITH 30% DEPOSIT, 70% AFTER RECEIPT OF FAXING COPY B/L</td></tr>
<tr><td>PORT OF LOADING:</td><td colspan="4">QINGDAO, CHINA</td></tr>
<tr><td>PORT OF DESTINATION:</td><td colspan="4">TORONTO, CANADA</td></tr>
<tr><td>TIME OF DELIVERY:</td><td colspan="4">WITHIN 30 DAYS AFTER RECEIPT OF 30% DEPOSIT</td></tr>
<tr><td rowspan="2">Marks and
Numbers</td><td>Description of goods</td><td>Quantity</td><td>Unit Price</td><td>Amount</td></tr>
<tr><td colspan="4" align="right">(CIF TORONTO)</td></tr>
<tr><td>MAPLE
TORONTO
NO. 1 – 100</td><td>ART. NO.
1 – 101 WOMEN'S
CASHMERE COATS
1 – 102 WOMEN'S
CASHMERE COATS
1 – 103 WOMEN'S
CASHMERE COATS</td><td>600PCS
200PCS
200PCS</td><td>USD100. 00/PC
USD90. 00/PC
USD90. 00/PC</td><td>USD60,000. 00
USD18,000. 00
USD18,000. 00</td></tr>
<tr><td></td><td></td><td colspan="2" align="center">TOTAL AMOUNT:</td><td><u>USD96,000. 00</u></td></tr>
<tr><td>TOTAL VALUE:</td><td colspan="4">SAY U. S. DOLLARS NINETY-SIX THOUSAND ONLY</td></tr>
<tr><td>BENEFICIARY:</td><td colspan="4">CAMELLIA GARMENTS CORPORATION
RM2901, SHANGRI-LA MANSION, 209 DONGHAI ROAD,
QINGDAO 266000, P. R. CHINA</td></tr>
<tr><td>ADVISING BANK:
A/C NO. :</td><td colspan="4">BANK OF CHINA, QINGDAO BRANCH
160 ZHONGSHAN ROAD, QINGDAO, CHINA
668763211866129

                         CAMELLIA GARMENTS CORPORATION
          RM2901, SHANGRI-LA MANSION, 209 DONGHAI ROAD
                    QINGDAO 266000, P. R. CHINA</td></tr>
</table>

Useful expressions

Sending Purchase Order (PO) 下订单
We have pleasure of placing the following order with you, and hope you kindly send the goods by fast freight. 非常高兴向你方订购以下商品，并希望贵方尽快发货。 Thank you for sending your catalogue and price list. We attach the order form and should be grateful if you would send the goods as soon as possible. 感谢你方寄来目录本和价目单。现随函寄去我们的订单，如你方能尽早发来货物，我们将不胜感激。 We are very pleased to have concluded this transaction. Kindly find our P/I attached and sign it back if everything is OK. 很高兴达成这笔交易，随信附寄形式发票，如无问题，敬请签字寄回。

Acceptance 接受订购
Thank you for your order for 100 metric tons of seamless steel pipes/tubes from us. 感谢你方向我方订购 100 公吨无缝钢管。 It is appreciated that you handed us your Order No. 123 for 2,500 women's shirts. 非常感谢贵方的 123 号订单向我们订购 2500 件女式衬衫。 With reference to your e-mail of December 4, we have pleasure in informing you that we have booked/accepted your order for 2,000 alarm clocks. 据贵方 12 月 4 日来信，我方很高兴通知贵方 2000 台闹钟订单已接受。 We are pleased to confirm having sold you 10,000 sets of Gree Air Conditioners. 我们很高兴确认向你方销售 10000 套格力空调。 We confirm supply of 10 tons green beans at EUR 3,000 per ton CFR Rotterdam for shipment in September. 我方确认向你方供应 10 吨绿豆，每吨 3000 欧元成本加运费鹿特丹，9 月份装运。

Countersignature 会签
We are sending/handing you our S/C No. 100 in duplicate, one copy of which please kindly sign/countersign and return for our file/record. 现寄我方第 100 号售货合同一式两份，一份签字后寄回，以便我方保存。 Attached please find the duplicate contract with our counter signature. 随函附上我方会签的一份合同，请查收。 We accept the order and are attaching you our Sales Confirmation No. 231 in triplicate of which please counter sign and return on copy to us for our file. 现随函附寄我方的 231 号销售确认书一式三份，请会签并寄回一份给我方以便存档。

Expectation 表示期盼

We trust that this initial order will lead to further dealings between our two companies.
我们相信这第一笔订单会使我们两家公司之间的生意源源不断。
If this first order is satisfactorily executed, we shall place further orders with you.
如果你方首次订货圆满执行，我方将大量订货。
Attached is a trial order. If the quality is up to our expectation, we shall send further orders in the near future.
我方随附试订单，如贵方产品质量达到我方期望，我方不久将有大量订货。
We intend to increase our order by 200 M/T copper concentrates. If this order is implemented smoothly, repeat orders will continuously come in.
我们想将订单增加 200 公吨铜矿砂。如果这笔首批订货交付顺利，后续订货将会源源而来。

Part 3 **Getting prepared for your task**

Ⅰ. Pattern drills. Make sentences with the following italicized expressions.

1. We are glad to *conclude the transaction of* 50,000 pieces of bed sheets.
(*to close/finalize/complete a deal...*)
A. 经过多轮商谈，我们最终达成了 1 万件风衣(trenches)的交易。
B. 买卖双方达成了一笔 5000 条紧身牛仔裤(skinny jeans)的交易。
C. 很高兴我们达成了 1000 件女士刺绣上衣(embroidered blouses)的交易。
D. 希望我们能尽早达成这笔 2 万双运动袜(sport socks)的交易。

2. We *confirm having booked your order for* 1,000 pieces of Women's Cashmere Coats.
A. 我方确认收到你方 2000 双耐克球鞋(sneakers)的订单。
B. 我方确认收到你方 5000 条黑色瑜伽裤(yoga leggings)的订单。
C. 我方确认收到你方 1000 件男士羽绒服(down jackets)的订单。
D. 我方确认收到你方 1000 副真皮手套(genuine leather gloves)的订单。

3. If this first order is satisfactorily executed, we shall *place further orders with you*.
A. 如果贵方产品质量达到我方期望，我方会再次订购。
B. 如果这笔订单交付顺利，我方会常年订购。
C. 如果贵方货品能令我方完全满意，我方会有续订购。
D. 如果产品销路好，我方会大量订购。

4. *Hope you kindly* send the goods by fast freight.
A. 希望你方收到货款后立即发货。
B. 希望你方按下列颜色搭配供货，红、黄、蓝、绿、棕色各 5 件。
C. 希望你方 5 天内安排发货。
D. 希望你方安排 10 月份发货。

II. Fill in the blanks with proper forms of the given expressions.

repeat order	supply sth from stock	execute	place an order
conclude	stipulations	for one's file	countersignature

1. We are glad to note that you have decided to _____ with us for 2,000 sets to test the market.

2. Please do your utmost to _____ this order for it will lead to more business.

3. There is an excessive demand for this item and we are not in a position to _____.

4. If the initial order proves satisfactory, we will place many _____.

5. All the _____ in the sales confirmation must be strictly observed by both parties of trade.

6. Attached please find our S/C No. ID472 in duplicate for your _____.

7. We are herein attaching our Purchase Contract No. 3674 in duplicate with our signature. Please countersign them and return one copy _____.

8. We are glad to have _____ deals with you on a wide variety of light industrial products.

III. Translate the following sentences into English.

1. 我们很高兴寄上 NT188 号销售合同一式两份，请你方签字并退回一份，以备我方存档。

2. 通过近期双方函电往来，我们很高兴与你方就 2000 双男士皮鞋达成交易。

3. 如果首批货物令我方客户满意，我们会大量续订。

4. 兹随附我方形式发票 83 号，请查收。

5. 我们很高兴地确认已从你方买进 50 套女童连衣裙，10 月份装运。

Part 4 Getting your task done

Now please write an e-mail, make out a proforma invoice and a sales contract based on your task in Part 1.

Attachment

PRO FORMA INVOICE				
TO:	DATE:			
	PI NO. :			
Term of Payment				
Port of Loading				
Port of Destination				
Time of Delivery				
Insurance				
Validity				
Marks and Numbers	Number and Kind of Packaging Description of Goods	Quantity	Unit Price	Amount
Total Amount:				
Say Total				
Beneficiary				
Advising Bank				
Negotiation Bank				

SALES CONTRACT			
SELLER	NO. :		
	DATE:		
BUYER	SIGNED IN:		
This contract is made by and agreed between the BUYER and SELLER, in accordance with the terms and conditions stipulated below.			
Commodity & Specification	Quantity	Unit Price & Trade Terms	Amount
Total			
Total Value			
Packaging			
Shipping Marks			
Time of Shipment & Means of Transportation			
Port of Loading & Destination			
Insurance			
Terms of Payment			
Remarks			
The Buyer (*signature*)		The Seller (*signature*)	

Task 12   Amending a Letter of Credit

LEARNING OBJECTIVES:

☞ To be able to find the discrepancies in an L/C, which are not in accordance with the contract stipulations

☞ To be able to write e-mails to notify your client to amend the discrepancies

Part 1   Getting to know your task

Scenario:

Shandong Tianyi Arts and Crafts Imp. & Exp. Corp. concludes a deal for dried flowers with FALCON ARTWORKS Co. Having checked the L/C No. 110LCI98546 issued by Bank of America, Houston, you find some items in the L/C not in accordance with the Purchase Order No. 1501.

Task 1:

Check the L/C below with the following purchase order, and then underline the discrepancies in the L/C.

Task 2:

You write an e-mail to Mr. Jonathan Porsche, the purchasing manager of FALCON ARTWORKS, and ask him to amend[1] the L/C.

FALCON ARTWORKS

PO BOX 1234 HOUSTON, TX USA 12345

TEL: 1 −713 −651 −6908 FAX: 1 −713 −651 −6906

PURCHASE ORDER

P/O No. 1501   DATE: AUG. 8, 20—

TO: SHANDONG TIANYI ARTS & CRAFTS IMP/EXP CO., LTD.

Art. No.	Descriptions	Unit Price FOB Qingdao	Quantity (PCS)	CTNS	Amount
BDF306	Bulk Dried Flower	USD9. 50/PC	500	50	USD4,750.00
JDF506	Jasmine Dried Flower	USD15. 10/PC	1,000	100	USD15,100.00
SDF608	Scented Dried Flower	USD1. 20/PC	6,000	600	USD7,200.00
TOTAL			7,500	750	USD27,050.00

1. SHIPPING MARKS：

> FA
> HOUSTON
> LOT NO. 1501

2. THE FOLLOWING DOCUMENTS MUST BE REQUIRED：
   (1) COMMERCIAL INVOICE
   (2) PACKING LIST
   (3) BILL OF LADING
   (4) CERTIFICATE OF ORIGIN
3. TIME OF SHIPMENT：OCTOBER 5，20--，WITH TRANSHIPMENT ALLOWED AND PARTIAL SHIPMENT NOT ALLOWED
4. DESTINATION PORT：HOUSTON，USA
5. TERMS OF PAYMENT：BY AN IRREVOCABLE L/C AT 30 DYAS AFTER SIGHT

****

中国银行
BANK OF CHINA

信用证通知书通知编号：AD98117

日期：20-- -09 -26

致：Shandong Tianyi Arts and Crafts Imp. & Exp. Corp.

65 Hongkong West Road，Qingdao，China

敬启者：

我行收到如下信用证一份：

开证行：Bank of America，Houston

开证日：20-- -09 -25

信用证号：110LCI98546

金额：USD 27,050.00

现随附通知。贵司交单时，请将本通知书及正本信用证一并提示。其他注意事项如下：

本信用证之通知系遵循国际商会《跟单信用证统一惯例》第 600 号出版物。

如有任何问题及疑虑，请与中国银行股份有限公司联络。

电话：0532 -82375943

传真：0532 -82370006

中国银行股份有限公司 MT：701

——ISSUE OF A DOCUMENTARY CREDIT——

SEQUENCE OF TOTAL：   27： 1/1
DOCUMENATRY CREDIT NUMBER：   20： 110LCI98546
DATE OF ISSUE：31C：150925
APPLICABLE RULES：40E：UCP LATEST VERSION
DATE AND PLACE OF EXPIRY：31D：151020 AT OUR COUNTER
APPLICANT：50C：FALCON ARTWORKS
HOUSTON, TX USA 12345
BENEFICIARY：59：SHANDONG TIANYI ARTS & CRAFTS IMP/EXP CO., LTD.
                    65 HONGKONG WEST ROAD QINGDAO, CHINA
CURRENCY CODE, AMOUNT：32B：USD 27050.00
AVAILABLE WITH...BY...：41D：AVAILABLE WITH
ANY BANKBY NEGOTIATION
DRAFTS AT...：42C：DRAFTS AT 60 DAYS AFTER SIGHT
DRAWEE：42D：OURSELVES
PARTIAL SHIPMENTS：43P：PARTIAL SHIPMENTS PROHIBITED
TRANSSHIPMENT：43T：TRANSHIPMENTS PROHIBITED
PORT OF LOADING/AIRPORT OF DEPARTURE：44E：ANY CHINESE PORT
PORT OF DISCHARGE/AIRPORT OF DESTINATION：44F：HOUSTON
LATEST DATE OF SHIPMENT：44C：151005
DESCRPT OF GOODS/SERVICES：45B：AS PER P/I NO. FA1501
DOCUMETNS REQUIRED：46A：
DOCUMENTS
COMMERCIAL INVOICE SIGNED AND STAMPED BY THE BENEFICIARY IN TRIPLI-
CATE
ORIGINAL CERTIFICATE OF ORIGIN IN DUPLICATE
PACKING LIST IN TRIPLICATE
3/3 ORIGINAL CLEAN ON BOARD MARINE/OCEAN BILLS OF LADING TO ORDER
BLANK ENDORSED MARKED FREIGHT PREPAID + 01 COPY NOTIFY APPLICA-
TION
INSURANCE POLICY OR CERTIFICATE
ADDITIONAL CONDITIONS：47B：
PAYMENT WITH RESERVES ARE NOT ALLOWED WITHOUT OUR PRIOR
AGREEMENT
CHARGES：71B：
ALL YOUR CHARGES FEES ARE TO BE FOR THE BENEFICIARY'S ACCOUNT

Brainstorming：

Make a list of discrepancies that may often occur in the L/C terms，which are not in accordance with the contract the seller and the buyer have agreed.

NOTES：

1. amend：*v.* 修改

Please amend your L/C to allow "Freight Prepaid".

请修改为"运费预付"。

Please amend the terms of payment to read "at 30 days after sight".

请将支付条款修改为见票后 30 天付款的远期信用证。

amendment：*n.* 改正；改善；改良

amendment to/of an L/C：对信用证的修改

amendment：*n.* 修改

We attach amendment advice No. QD003 to L/C No. CR - 57. Please find it in order.

兹附上第 CR - 57 号信用证的第 QD003 修改通知书，请查收。

Part 2 | Learning about a similar task ▷▷ ▷▷ ▷▷

Sample e-mail 1：Amending an L/C（1）

From：alexanderlee @ dpoan. com
To：harryhill@ weekend. com
Date：Sept 5th, 20--
Subject：Amending L/C No. LC436/2090/166C

Dear Harry Hill,

We have received your L/C No. LC436/2090/166C for Contract No. TY709.

We find it contains the following discrepancies and would request you to make the following amendments：

1. Owing to the delay of the L/C, the validity[1] of the L/C should be extended to Nov. 15th.
2. Please insert "TRANSSHIPMENT AND PARTIALSHIPMENT ALLOWED" as we agreed in the contract.
3. Inspection Certificate[2] should be issued by the Tianjin Commodity Inspection Bureau[3] instead of Qingdao Commodity Inspection Bureau.
4. Please delete your request for insurance policy/certificate.

Please see to it that the L/C amendment reaches us before Sept 25th. Otherwise, we will not be able to effect shipment in time.

Looking forward to receiving your L/C amendment early.

Best regards,
Alexander Lee

NOTES:

1. validity: *n.* 有效期

Please extend your L/C validity till May 15, 20--.

请将信用证的有效期延长到20--年的5月15日。

2. Inspection Certificate: 检验证明书

3. Commodity Inspection Bureau: 商品检验局

Sample e-mail 2: Amending an L/C (2)

From: thomasanderson @ elange. com
To: purchasing@ staring. com
Date: Sept 5th, 20--
Subject: Amending L/C No. LC475HGM012

Dear Wendy,

We are very pleased to receive your L/C No. 475HGM012 issued by THE BANK OF CHINA, LTD. NEW YORK AGENCY 79 BROADWAY NEW YORK, N. Y. 10005 DATED FEB 12. 20--.

But the following points do not conform to the stipulations[1] of our S/C No. 90CHET179. Please amend the L/C as follows:

1. Please extend[2] the shipment date and the validity of the L/C to Nov. 15th and Nov. 25th respectively[3].
2. As there are no direct steamers sailing to your port next month, please amend the relative clause to read[4] "transshipment allowed".

Thank you for your kind cooperation. Please see to it that[5] the L/C amendment reaches us before Sept. 25th, otherwise we shall not be able to effect punctual[6] shipment.

Best regards,
Thomas Anderson

NOTES：

1. stipulation：*n.* 约束，契约，约定

It goes against the stipulations of the contract to insure the goods for 130% of the invoice value.
按发票金额的 130% 给货物投保是违背合同规定的。

2. extend：*v.* 延长，宽延；扩展

We propose that you extend the L/C to Oct. 30 to avoid the possible delay in shipment.
为避免延误装运，建议你方将信用证延至 10 月 30 号。

Your bank might agree to extend the period of the loan for six months.
你的银行可能会同意延长贷款期限 6 个月。

3. respectively：*adv.* 分别地，各自地

We received payments of ＄275 on the 2nd July, and ＄525 on the 9th July respectively.
我方分别在 7 月 2 日和 7 月 9 日收到 275 美元和 525 美元两笔付款。

4. read：*v.* 读作，内容是

The L/C number should read LC5041757119 instead of LC5641757119.
信用证号应为 LC5041757119 而不是 LC5641757119。

5. see (to it) that...：务请注意(做到)，确保，设法使，留意做到

that 从句中要用一般现在时

Please see that all the goods against Order No. 125 are packed in cartons.
务请注意订单 125 号项下的所有货物用纸板箱包装。

We will see to it that we send you a full range of samples by DHL.
我们会用敦豪快递寄去全套样品。

6. punctual：*adj.* 严守时刻的，准时的

When we placed the order, we pointed out that punctual shipment was of utmost importance.
我们在订货时就指出，准时装运是极为重要的。

Useful expressions

Acknowledging receipt of L/C 告知来证
Thank you for your L/C No. 789/267 issued by the Bank of China, Madrid Branch dated 25th May, 20—.   感谢贵方由中国银行马德里分行 20— 年 5 月 25 日开立的 789/267 号信用证。   We are pleased to receive L/C No. 477/30D established by HSBC, Osaka Branch dated March 31, 20— under S/C No. 787DC3.   感谢收到 787DC3 号合同项下由汇丰银行大阪分行 20— 年 3 月 31 日开立的 477/30D 号信用证。

Listing points of discrepancies 列明不符点
We are sorry to find it contains the following discrepancies. 很遗憾发现信用证存在下列不符之处。 Please amend the price clause to read "CFR London". 请将价格条款更改为 CFR London。 Please insert the word "about" before the quantity and amount in your L/C. 请在信用证数量和金额前增加"大约"二字。 Please amend your L/C to "allow partial shipment and transshipment". 请在信用证中修改装运条款为"允许分批装运和转运"。 Please amend "Freight Collect" to read "Freight Prepaid". 请将运费到付改为运费预付。 The amount should be ＄459,000 instead of ＄439,000. 总金额应为 459000 美元，而不是 439000 美元。 Please increase the amount to USD50,100. 请将金额增加至 50100 美元。
Asking for prompt amendment 催促更改
We hope you will send the amendment without delay. 希望贵方务必及时将修订件寄送我方。 As the time of shipment is approaching, please make the necessary amendments the soonest possible so that we can effect shipment in time. 由于装运时间临近，请尽快完成必要修改，以便我方及时发货。

Part 3   Getting prepared for your task

Ⅰ. Pattern drills. Make sentences with the following italicized expressions.

1. As there are no direct steamers sailing to your port next month, please *amend* the relative clause *to read* "transshipment allowed".

A. 请将第 1200 号信用证中的订购数量由 5 箱更改为 10 箱，其余部分不变。

B. 请要求银行将第 45 号信用证修改为"接受第 48 号信用证下联运提单"。

C. 请按照合同将总金额修改为"三百七十六万美元整"。

D. 请将受益人名字改为"津津股份有限公司"，而不是"亲亲股份有限公司"。

2. In order to avoid subsequent amendments, please *see to it* that the L/C stipulation conforms to the terms of the Contract.

A. 请确保货物由 10 月 15 日左右起航的"胜利轮"装运。

B. 请确保你方信用证在下月初开出，而且准许分批装运和转船。

C. 请确保我方所订货物在有关信用证抵达贵方时立即装船。

D. 请确保此货要在 5 月 15 日前装运并按发票金额 150% 投保一切险。

3. *Owing to* the delay of the L/C, the validity of the L/C should be extended to Nov. 15th.

A. 由于价格上的分歧，我们不得不终止此次谈判。

B. 由于缺少直航班轮，我们要求允许进行转运。

C. 由于产品上市的时间安排较紧，请在收到信用证的 30 天内发货。

D. 由于开证延误，装运无法按合同规定的时间完成，需延期到 10 月份。

Ⅱ. Fill the blanks with the following given words.

request	instead of	validity	negotiation	discrepancy
amendment	see to it	issue	punctual	respectively

Dear Mr. Stephenson,

We have received your L/C No. 567/23 _____ by the Agricultural Bank of China Beijing Branch for the amount of $23,120 covering 1,200 pairs of sneakers.

After reviewing the L/C, we find it contains the following _____ and would _____ you to make the following _____:

1. The credit is to be valid for _____ in China _____ in Italy.

2. Please extend the shipment date and the _____ of the L/C to June 10th and June. 25th _____.

Thank you for your kind cooperation, please _____ that the L/C amendment reaches us before Feb. 25th, otherwise we shall not be able to effect _____ shipment.

Best regards,

Jane McDonald

Ⅲ. Make sentences based on the following scenario.

Marvin Arthurhas received an L/C which contains some discrepancies against the contract. He has marked the mistakes and indicated the correct information. Write four complete sentences to inform the buyers of the discrepancies and ask them to make amendments.

Contract Number	76890
Seller	Muses Export Ltd.
Buyer	J&M Ltd.
Product	SBW32 BASKETBALL
Quantity	1,500 (2,500)
Price	USD4,500 FOB Shanghai (7,500)
Port of loading and destination	From Shanghai to Vancouver with transshipment and partial shipment prohibited. (allowed)

Time of shipment	During Mar. 20--
Payment	100% confirmed and irrevocable Letter of Credit opened by the buyer, valid for negotiation in Canada 45 days after shipment. (China)

1. _____
2. _____
3. _____
4. _____

Part 4   Getting your task done

Now please underline the discrepancies in the L/C based on your Task 1 and then write an e-mail based on your Task 2 in Part 1.

Task 13　Handling Shipment Issues

LEARNING OBJECTIVES:

☞ To be able to write a shipping advice, informing the client of shipping arrangement

☞ To be able to write e-mails, asking the client to accept changes to the shipping arrangement

Part 1　Getting to know your task

Scenario:

TJ Max Homeware purchases some women's sweaters from Bloom Garments Co. on FOB terms. The order is to be paid by T/T with 30% in advance and 70% after shipment against shipping documents. Now, the goods ordered have been loaded on board S. S MUSES M. 223 on Oct. 5. The detailed information is as follows:

1. INVOICE NO.: TD03257
2. DESCRIPTION OF GOODS: WOMEN'S SWEATER 4,500 PCS
3. BILL OF LADING[1] NO.: TD214567
4. OCEAN VESSEL: MUSES M. 223
5. ETD[2]: on or about Oct. 7
6. ETA[3]: on or about Oct. 25
7. Port of destination: London, UK
8. Shipping Agency[4] at port of destination: Damco Solutions Ltd.

84 Uxbridge Road,

Ealing, London W13 8RA

Phone: +44 208 799 2800

Fax: +44 208 090 6201

Task:

Write a shipping advice[5] on behalf of the seller to Charles J. Orlando, purchase manager of TJ MAX Homeware, containing the information mentioned above.

Brainstorming:

Why is it necessary for the seller to send a shipping advice after the shipment is completed? Besides the information mentioned in the scenario, what else can the seller provide to the buyer?

NOTES:

1. bill of lading: 提单
主要的提单类型包括:

on board B/L 已装船提单   open B/L 不记名提单

transhipment B/L 转船提单   straight B/L 记名提单

clean B/L 清洁提单   direct B/L 直达提单

unclean B/L 不清洁提单   through B/L 联运提单

foul B/L 不清洁提单

2. ETD: Estimated Time of Departure 预计离港时间
3. ETA: Estimated Time of Arrival 预计抵达时间
4. shipping agency: 货运代理, 又叫 forwarding agency, 或者 forwarder
5. shipping advice: 装船通知

Part 2   Learning about a similar task

Sample e-mail 1: Shipping advice (1)

From: jesse_woods@ teeya. com
To: jonathanhunter@ dkke. com
Date: Sept 5th, 20--
Subject: Shipping advice for P/I No. 793D
Dear Mr. Hunter, We acknowledge[1] receipt of your L/C No. 230/77C. We are pleased to inform you that the goods under Proforma Invoice No. 793D have been shipped on S. S. Tethys[2] due to[3] sail for Madrid[4] on June 5th. Please find the details as follows:

Commodity：silk flowers

Quantity：150 cartons

Amount：USD10,250.00

Invoice No. ：793D

Total G. W. ：750kg

Name of vessel：Tethys

Voy. No. [5]：M－238

Port of lading：Danang, Vietnam[6]

Port of destination：Madrid, Spain

ETD：June 5, 20－－

ETA：June 25, 20－－

B/L NO. ：BL6890C

Insurance policy No. 898

We hope the said goods will reach you in due time[7]. Thank you for your kind cooperation, and we are looking forward to your future orders.

Best regards,

Jesse Woods

NOTES：

1. acknowledge：*v.* 承认，认可……属实或存在

We will acknowledge receipt of your order.

兹告，已收到你方订单。

She acknowledged having been at fault.

她承认自己有过错。

She acknowledged that she had been at fault.

她承认自己有过错。

2. shipped on（board）S. S. Tethys：装上"特提斯"号轮

S. S. ：steamship 汽船，泛指船

还可缩写为 s. s. 或 S/S，后面跟船名，如 S. S. Victoria "维多利亚"号轮

还常用 M. V. 或者 m. v. ，即 motor vessel 轮船的缩写。

"由……轮运输"可以表达为：

shipped by/per... 由……轮装运/运出

shipped ex... 由……轮运来

This is to inform you that your order has been shipped by/per S. S. "Queen".

兹告你方订货已由"皇后"号轮运出。

20 cartons out of shipment ex/by S. S. "Queen" were found broken.

由"皇后"号轮运来的货物中有 20 箱破损。

3. due to：(按计划)定于……

The tax hearing is due to begin next month.

税务问题听证会定于下月召开。

4. sail for Madrid：驶往马德里港口

sail：*v.* 航行；起航(for/to)

The goods have been loaded on board S. S. "Red Star", which is due to sail from Qingdao to Copenhagen on or about April 7.

货物已装到红星轮上，该轮定于 4 月 7 号左右由青岛开往哥本哈根。

sailing date 起航期

5. Voy. No.：航次 Voyage Number

6. Danang, Vietnam：越南岘港

7. in due time：如期地，适时地

Sample e-mail 2：Shipping advice（2）

From：tong_zhang@ cherry. com
To：peterhale@ joyart. com
Date：Oct. 14th, 20--
Subject：Shipping advice for Order No. 06002850023
Dear Mr. Hale, We are pleased to tell you we have dispatched your Order No. 06002850023 by DHL. You can track[1] its progress with the following tracking number：2045156988. You can also track the delivery of your order yourself here： 　http：//www. dhl. com/en/express/tracking. html. It usually takes about 5 days for your order to arrive, but as this is the shopping season, the logistics companies[2] are very busy and some orders may take slightly longer to arrive. If you have any questions or problems, contact us directly for help. Best regards, Tong Zhang

NOTES：

1. track：*v.* 追踪

You may log in to track the status of your shipments.

你可以登录以追踪货物运输状态。

2. logistics company：物流公司

Sample e-mail 3：Shipment delay and partial shipment

From：isaac. m @ BPHF. com
To：ss_brown @ mile. com
Date：May 5th, 20—
Subject：Shipment delay
Dear Ms. Brown,   We have received your e-mail of 3rd May requiring us to ship 1, 200 sets of high-fidelity audio equipment[1] before 1st June.   We regret to inform you that the production has been delayed due to an industrial dispute[2] last month. Therefore we are not able to ship the goods in one lot.   May I have your permission to make the shipment in three equal lots? In that case, the first lot is expected to reach your port at the end of this month, and the 2nd and the 3rd lot in mid-June and late June respectively.   We are very sorry for the inconvenience[3] and await your early reply.   Best regards,   Isaac Miller

NOTES：

1. high-fidelity audio equipment：高保真音响

2. industrial dispute：劳资纠纷

3. inconvenience：*n.* 不便

We apologize for any inconvenience caused during the repairs.

我们为维修期间造成的任何不便道歉。

Sample e-mail 4: Extending delivery time

From: tong_zhang@cherry.com
To: peter_hale@joyart.com
Date: Nov. 10th, 20--
Subject: Shipping advice for Order No. 06002850023

Dear Mr. Hale,

We have checked the tracking information and found your package is still in transit[1].
This is due to the overwhelming demand[2] for logistics this shopping season. In this case, we are sorry to inform you that the package will probably arrive 10 days later than expected. We have also extended the time period for you to confirm delivery.

Please don't worry about your money or your purchase. If you do not receive your package, we will resend your order, or you can apply for a full refund[3].

Thanks for your understanding.

Best regards,
Tong Zhang

NOTES:

1. in transit: 在运输途中
2. overwhelming demand: 势不可挡的需求
3. refund: *n. v.* 退款
full refund: 全额退款
I took the laptop back to the shop and asked for a refund.
我把手提电脑拿回商店，要求店方退款。
We guarantee to refund you the full price if you're not delighted with your purchase.
如果你对购买的商品不满意，我们保证全额退款。

Useful expressions

Advising shipment 告知发货
We are pleased to inform you that the following goods have been shipped on S. S. Liberty. 我们很高兴地通知贵方，下列货物已由"自由号"货轮发出。 We are pleased to inform you that your order has been shipped per/by S. S. Earl.

欣告你方订货已由"伯爵"号轮运出。

This is to notify you that we have shipped 20 cartons of toys, which are expected to reach Nagoya on March 3rd.

现通知贵方，我方已将 20 箱玩具发出，预计 3 月 3 日到达名古屋。

Asking for changing mode of shipment or date of shipment
要求更改运输方式或时间

As there are no direct steamers available this month, we'd like to ask you to extend the shipment date to June 10th.

因为本月没有直达班轮，我方要求将装运时间延长到 6 月 10 日。

As the only direct steamer which calls on our port once a month has just departed, goods can only be shipped next month.

由于每一月抵港的直接船已起航，货只能下月装运。

Shipment could be made in September, provided that transshipment is allowed.

如果允许转运，9 月即可发货。

Other useful expressions 其他常用表达

The shipment time is February or March at our option and the goods will be shipped in one lot.

装运期为 2 月或 3 月，由我方决定，货物将一批装完。

We shall effect shipment in May provided your letter of credit reaches here before the 15th April.

我们可于 5 月装货，但信用证必须于 4 月 15 日前到达。

Owing to the late arrival of your L/C, shipment cannot be effected as stipulated.

由于贵方信用证延迟的原因，无法如约发货。

The said goods will reach you in perfect condition.

上述货物将完好的送达贵方。

Shipment is to be made from March in three equal lots with transshipment at Colombo.

货物将从 3 月开始，分 3 次均装，在科伦坡转船。

Goods will be shipped within 30 days after receipt of your L/C.

货可于收到贵方信用证后 30 天内装出。

We will airmail you original documents upon receipt of balance payment.

收到余款后，我方将航寄单据正本给贵方。

Part 3 Getting prepared for your task

Ⅰ. Pattern drills. Make sentences with the following italicized expressions.

1. *May I have your permission to* ship the 3,000 dozen blouses in three equal lots?

A. 请允许我在收到贵方信用证的 30 天内发货。

B. 请允许我向您解释一下此次发货延期的原因。

C. 由于直航班轮数量较少，请允许我方在新加坡转运货物。

D. 由于不可抗力，请允许我单方面取消此次机械设备购买合同。

2. The goods have long been ready for shipment, but owing to the late arrival of your L/C, shipment cannot be effected *as stipulated*.

A. 担保函必须在合同规定的装运期前两个月到达我方。

B. 我们保证货物符合合同中所订购的规格。

C. 根据合同规定，付款条件应为即期信用证而不是即期付款交单。

D. 卖方不应对下述规定的不可抗力导致的货物延迟或未能交付承担责任。

3. Shipment can be effected within two or three weeks *after receipt of* your L/C.

A. 收到贵公司的订单后，我公司将在两周内交货。

B. 收到可以转船及分批装运之信用证后 15 天内装出。

C. 收到汇款后，我方将立即支付 3% 的佣金。

D. 请注意这订单的出货将在收到贵方的信用证之后 60 天之内。

Ⅱ. Fill the missing words in the blanks.

ensure	equal	direct
respectively	confirm	transshipped

Dear Mr. Field,

We have received your e-mail of 10ᵗʰ September, asking us to ship the goods in two _____ lots in November and December _____.

We wish to inform you that _____ sailings for your port are few and far between. To _____ that the products are launched before Christmas, we propose that they be _____ at Madrid.

Please _____ by e-mail so that we can make necessary arrangement with our shipping company.

Best regards,
Ian Carl

Ⅲ. Translate the following sentences into Chinese.

1. 兹告知收到贵方 5 月 30 日关于 1358 号订单的邮件。

2. 很高兴地通知你方，你的货物已于 3 月 29 日由"自由号"货轮送出，预计 4 月 12 日抵达墨尔本。

3. 由于 11 月底之前所有直达轮都已满仓，我方无法按约定时间发货。

4. 我方提议装运从 7 月开始，分两次均装，在大阪(Osaka)转船。

5. 由于购物旺季物流公司业务繁忙，贵方订货未能如期发出，为此我们感到十分抱歉。

Ⅳ. Translate the following e-mail into Chinese.

Dear Tony,

As we all know, it's the busiest part of the shopping season and the international couriers are running at maximum capacity.

Your delivery information has not been updated yet, but don't worry, we will let you know as soon as an update is available.

Thank you for your patience.

Best regards,
Blair

Part 4 Getting your task done

Please write a shipping advice based on your task in Part 1.

Task 14　Urging for Payment of Balance Due

LEARNING OBJECTIVE:

☞ To be able to write e-mails asking customers to pay the balance due

Part 1　Getting to know your task

Scenario:

Tony Yang is the sales manager of Rush Outdoor Wares[1] Corp. According to the Proforma Invoice #345 – RP below with Stars Imp. & Exp. Co., Ltd., the goods have been dispatched and will be arriving at New York soon. However, Tony hasn't received the payment of balance.

Task:

Write an e-mail on behalf of Tony Yang to Rubio, salesman from Stars Imp. & Exp. Co., Ltd., to ask him to finish the payment a. s. a. p.

<table>
<tr><td colspan="5" align="center">RUSH OUTDOOR WARES CORPORATION
18/F, Sunshine Bldg., 718 Nanjing East Road, Shanghai 200003, P. R. China
TEL: 021 – 63526637　　FAX: 021 – 63526638</td></tr>
<tr><td colspan="5" align="center">PROFORMA INVOICE</td></tr>
<tr><td colspan="3">TO: STARS IMP. & EXP. CO., LTD</td><td colspan="2">INVOICE NO.　#345 – RP</td></tr>
<tr><td colspan="2">184 JAMAICA AV HOLLIOS NY 11423, USA</td><td>INVOICE DATE</td><td colspan="2">MAR. 17, 20—</td></tr>
<tr><td colspan="2">TERMS OF PAYMENT:</td><td colspan="3">BY T/T WITH 30% DEPOSIT, 70% AFTER RECEIPT OF FAXING COPY OF B/L</td></tr>
<tr><td colspan="2">PORT OF LOADING:</td><td colspan="3">SHANGHAI, CHINA</td></tr>
<tr><td colspan="2">PORT OF DESTINATION:</td><td colspan="3">NEW YORK, USA</td></tr>
<tr><td colspan="2">TIME OF DELIVERY:</td><td colspan="3">WITHIN 30 DAYS AFTER RECEIPT OF 30% DEPOSIT</td></tr>
<tr><td>Marks and
Numbers</td><td>Description of goods
ART. NO.</td><td>Quantity</td><td>Unit Price
(CIF NEW
YORK)</td><td>Amount</td></tr>
</table>

STARS USA NO. 1–150	ISB01INFLATABLE SLEEPING BAGS[2] ISB02INFLATABLE SLEEPING BAGS ISB03INFLATABLE SLEEPING BAGS	1000 PCS 2000 PCS 2000 PCS	USD5. 80/PC USD4. 90/PC USD4. 10/PC	USD5,800. 00 USD9,800. 00 USD8,200. 00
		TOTAL AMOUNT：		USD23,800. 00
TOTAL VALUE：	SAY U. S. DOLLARS TWENTY-THREE THOUSAND EIGHT HUNDRED ONLY			
BENEFICIARY：	RUSH OUTDOOR WARES CORPORATION 18/F, Sunshine Bldg., 718 Nanjing East Road, Shanghai 200003, P. R. CHINA			
ADVISING BANK： A/C NO. ：	BANK OF CHINA, SHANGHAI BRANCH 231 NANJING EAST ROAD, SHANGHAI, P. R. CHINA 689372612488157 RUSH OUTDOOR WARES CORPORATION 18/F, Sunshine Bldg., 718 Nanjing East Road, Shanghai 200003, P. R. CHINA			

Brainstorming：

At what stage of a business transaction should the sellers ask the buyers to pay the balance?

NOTES：

1. outdoor ware：户外用品

2. inflatable sleeping bag：充气睡袋

Part 2　Learning about a similar task

Sample e-mail 1：Urging for the payment of balance due

From：emma. wu@ toysworld. com
To：johncruz@ joy. com
Subject：Balance due
Dear John, Hope this e-mail finds you well.[1] As arranged in our order #203TY, the balance (70% of the total amount, i. e. USD81,300) should be paid by T/T against the copy of B/L. However, we haven't got your payment of the balance due[2] yet. As the goods will be arriving at your port in a couple of days, please expedite[3] the payment to avoid unnecessary port charges caused by the potential delay.

Once we get your evidence of remittance[4], we'll release[5] the original B/L to you.

Regards,

Emma

NOTES：

1. Hope this E-mail finds you well. ：见信安好

2. due：*adj.* 到期的，应付的

balance due：应付余款

The first payment is due.

首期款到期(应付)了。

The rent is due at the end of the month.

租金应在月底交。

overdue：*adj.* 过期的

Your payment has been long overdue.

你方付款已逾期已久。

3. expedite *v.* 加快进展；迅速完成

相当于 speed up, hasten

We will expedite shipment as soon as possible.

我们将尽可能加速装运。

4. evidence of remittance：汇款凭证

5. release：*v.* 放出，发出

express release bill of lading：电放填单

delivery release：发货通知

freight release：放货通知，船货放行单

Sample e-mail 2：A reply to the above

From：johncruz@ joy. com
To：emma. wu@ toysworld. com
Subject：Re：Balance due
Attachment：bank receipt. jpg(10K)
Dear Emma, I apologize for our one week delay in payment. The remittance was made for USD81,300 today, and the bank receipt[1] is attached as requested.

Please confirm with us when you've got the money and send me the original B/L.

Have a nice day.

John

NOTES：

1. bank receipt：水单，即汇款后银行给的留底凭条，也可以叫作 bank slip

Sample e-mail 3：Insufficient[1] payment

| From：graceqin@ luckybros. com |
| To：thomas@ gifts. com |
| Subject：Order #RT45 |
| Attachment：Order #RT45. pdf（1. 2M） |

Dear Thomas，

We got your payment by PayPal[2] this morning for USD1,074 with thanks. However, the total for your order # RT45 as attached is USD1,095. So there is a balance of ＄21.

It is our customary practice that we arrange shipment when receiving your full payment. So please kindly pay the balance ＄21. We'll arrange shipment and let you know the tracking number on receipt of the balance.

Your understanding and attention[3] will be much appreciated.

Best wishes，

Grace

NOTES：

1. insufficient：adj. 不足的
2. PayPal：贝宝，PayPal 是一种国际贸易支付方式，即时支付，即时到账，免费注册，交易时收取一定数额的手续费。
3. attention：n. 关注，此处可以理解为"办理，处理"。

Useful expressions

| Urging payment 催促付款 |
| Please prepay 30% of the total amount to us, and then kindly remit us the balance before the delivery.
请预付给我方总金额的30%，并于交货前汇付余款。
Please transfer the remaining US＄1,500 repairing fee to the following account. |

请将余下的 1500 美元的维修费转账至下面的账户。

We propose to give you 15 days to clear your account.

我们再给你们 15 天来结清账目。

The following items totaling ＄4,000 are still open on your account.

你以下货品的欠款总计为 4000 美元。

Several weeks have passed since we sent you our first invoice and we have not yet received your payment.

我们的第一份发票已经寄出有好几周了，但我们尚未收到你的任何款项。

I'm wondering about your plans for paying your account which, as you know, has been overdue for 40 days.

我想了解一下你的付款计划，要知道，你的付款已经逾期 40 多天了。

We must now ask you to settle this account within the next few days.

现在我们不得不要求你方在几天内结清账目。

Since the account is long overdue, we would very much appreciate your prompt processing of payment on your side.

由于该款逾期已久，我们将万分感谢你们立即处理付款事宜。

We would appreciate a prompt settlement of this account.

我们将非常感谢你们迅速结清此账。

Notifying payment 通知已付款
As agreed, we have remitted you the full amount of the goods by T/T. 按照约定，我们已将货物总额电汇给了你方。 Please note that the previous outstanding balance has been repaid in full. 请注意以前的未清余额已全部结清。

Balance 余款
We have received payments of ＄275 on the 2nd July, and ＄525 on the 9th July respectively. This leaves a debit balance of ＄320. 我们分别在 7 月 2 日和 7 月 9 日收到 275 美元和 525 美元两笔付款。这样还剩下欠款余额 320 美元。 The outstanding balance in this order is ＄500 in total. 该订单未结清余额达到了 500 美元。

Part 3 Getting prepared for your task

Ⅰ. Pattern drills. Make sentences with the following italicized expressions.

1. *Hope* this e-mail *finds you well*.

A. 谨以此信(letter)向您致以问候。

B. 谨以此便条(note)向您致以问候。

C. 谨以此消息(message)向您致以问候。

2. *Please confirm with us* when you've got the money.

A. 当新原料到货时，请跟我方确认一下。

B. 请确认客户样品是否可以生产。

C. 余款是否结清，请确认。

D. 如客户接受对标签设计的更改，请与我方确认。

3. *It is our customary practice that* we arrange shipment when receiving your full payment.

A. 我们的惯例是，这种货品最低起订量是 1000 件。

B. 我们的惯例是，由客户承担样品费和邮资。

C. 我们的惯例是，对新客户要求采用信用证的支付方式。

D. 我们的惯例是，在开始投入生产前电汇预付 30%，余款见提单复印件付清。

4. *Please kindly* finish the balance ＄21.

A. 敬请查收附件的电子表格。

B. 敬请告知此安排是否可行。

C. 敬请注意(be informed)，货物不一定能在 10 号到港。

D. 敬请留意，你方所订货物已装运。

Ⅱ. Fill in the blanks with proper forms of the following expressions and then put the e-mail into Chinese.

balance	as follows	remit	total amount
attention	regarding	appreciate	quantity

Dear Mr. Grind,

Thank you for your order for cotton sheets. _____ 4,500 pcs, the details are _____ :

Commodity：All Cotton Bed Sheets（Woven）ART#6302

    _____ : 4,500 pcs

  Unit price：at USD5. 76/pc FOB Qingdao

    _____ : USD25,920. 00

We have yourc heck for USD20,000 which we will hold until you _____ the _____ of USD 5,920. The rest of the cotton sheets will then be dispatched.

Your immediate _____ will be much _____.

Yours truly,

Eric

Ⅲ. Put the following e-mail into English.

催款函主题：索取逾期账款

Mike，您好！

鉴于贵方总是及时结清项目，而此次逾期一个月仍未收到贵方上述账目的欠款，我们想知道是否有何特殊原因。

我们猜想贵方可能未及时收到我们8月30日发出的80000美元欠款的账单。现寄出一份，并希望贵方及早处理。

你真诚的 May

Part 4   Getting your task done

Now please write an e-mail based on your task in Part 1.

Task 15   Handling Customer Complaints

LEARNING OBJECTIVE:

☞ To be able to write e-mails handling customer complaints and claims

Part 1   Getting to know your task

Scenario:

Christa Koch, the Head of Textile Division of Adecco Trading Corporationin Zurich, Switzerland, has purchased 1,000 pieces of Baby Girl Pullovers[1] from Qingdao Vatrad Group Co., Ltd. She complains[2] that the Baby Girl Pullovers Art. No. 8954.079 are full of holes after just one wash. They have to withdraw[3] this article from their stores due to too many customer claims[4]. She asks Tina Feng, the Export Manager of Qingdao Vatrad Group Co., Ltd., to give her an explanation, and lodges a claim for USD30,659. Attached is a Survey Report[5] in support of her statement.

Task:

Write an e-mail of settlement[6] to Christa Koch on behalf of Tina Feng in response to Christa Koch's complaint by offering reasonable solutions.

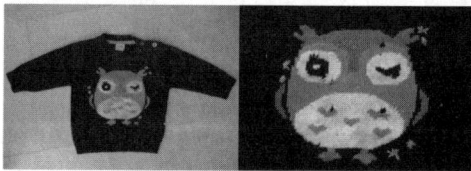

(Before Wash)

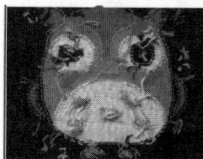

(After Wash)

Brainstorming：

When a customer lodges a complaint, what is considered to be important for a company to do?

NOTES：

1. Baby Girl Pullover：女婴套头衫

2. complain：*v.* 投诉，抱怨

complain to sb. of/about sth. 因……向……抱怨

We have to complain to you of the delay in shipment which has caused us much trouble.
我方不得不对你方推迟发货给我们造成的不便表示不满。

complain that... 抱怨……

We regret to complain that your consignment of sweaters does not conform to the samples, either in quality or in color.
我方抱歉投诉你方的毛衣质量和颜色与样品不符。

complaint：*n.* 投诉，抱怨

make/lodge/lay/file a complaint with sb. about sth. 因……向……抱怨

The importer has filed a complaint with our corporation about poor packaging of the goods.
进口商已经就货物的不良包装向我们公司投诉。

3. withdraw：*v.* 撤回

4. claim：*n. v.* 索赔

lodge/file/raise/put in a claim 提出索赔

claim against sb. 向某人索赔

claim on sth. 为某货物索赔

claim for 为某原因索赔

claim for 索赔……金额

We have to lodge a claim against you on this shipment for USD2,100 for short weight.
恐怕我方必须对你方这批船货向你提出短重索赔2100美元。

5. Survey Report 检验报告

6. settlement：*n.* 处理

settlement of a claim 理赔

We have arranged for the replacement to be dispatched to you in settlement of your claim.
我方已经安排寄送替代品给你方进行理赔。

settle：*v.* 处理

settle a claim 理赔

We encounter difficulties in settling the claim.
理赔时我们遇到了困难。

Part 2 Learning about a similar task

Sample e-mail 1: Settling a claim for inferior quality

From: annie@ china-garlic. cn
To: anthonymaloney@ gmail. com
Date: Oct. 23, 20--
Subject: Re: Claim for fresh white garlic
Dear Mr. Maloney,   We are sorry to learn from your e-mail of October 22, 20-- claiming for inferior[1] quality on the consignment[2] of 500 metric tons of fresh white garlic[3], some of which has gone mouldy[4].   We wish to express our deep regret at this incident[5]. We have checked with our warehouse[6] and discovered that part of your consignment was not stored and transported with a temperature of $-3°C$ as specified in the contract[7]. This was due to the negligence[8] of our warehouse staff.   We fully understand your present situation. If you agree, we will offer you a 5% discount for your next order. Please let me know whether this is agreeable to you.   We apologize[9] for the trouble caused and hope you will grant us further opportunity to regain your confidence[10].   Best regards,   Annie Zhang

NOTES:

1. inferior: *adj.* 低劣的

Please send us the sample of inferior goods for examination.

请把次品的样品发来供我方检查。

Synthetic fabric is inferior to cotton fabric.

合成纤维织物不如棉织品好。

2. consignment: *n.* 货物

3. fresh white garlic: 新鲜白蒜

4. mouldy: *adj.* 发霉的

5. incident：*n.* 事件

6. warehouse：*n.* 仓库

7. as specified in the contract：按合同规定

8. negligence：*n.* 疏忽，粗心大意

9. apologize：*v.* 道歉

apologize to sb. for sth. 因……向……道歉

We apologize to you for this unfortunate matter.

对于这一不幸事件，我方向你方表示歉意。

apology：*n.* 道歉

Please accept our apology for the delay in reply to your e-mail of June 8.

迟迟未回复你方6月8日邮件，请接受我方的道歉。

Trains may be subject to delay—we apologize for any inconvenience caused.

列车可能会延误，如果给您造成任何不便，我们在此谨致歉意。

10. regain your confidence：恢复您的信心

Sample e-mail 2：Settling a claim for short delivery

From：maggie@ tabocandles. com
To：miller@ pillartrading. com
Date：Sept. 18，20--
Subject：About the short delivery of Order No. 54621
Dear Mr. Miller,   We have received your e-mail of September 17，20-- , in which you informed us of the short delivery[1] of 100 sets of your LED candles with remote controls[2] under Order No. 54621.   On going into[3] this matter thoroughly, we found that the shortage was caused by the oversight[4] of the worker packing the goods. We regret the negligence on our side and have dispatched[5] another lot of 100 sets of LED candles with remote controls to you. They will reach you within one week.   We apologize for the inconvenience incurred and would like to assure you that similar mistakes will be avoided[6] in the handling of your future orders.   Best regards,   Maggie Xu

NOTES：

1. short delivery：短交

2. LED candle with remote control：远程遥控 LED 蜡烛

3. go into：调查

Please be assured that we will go into the matter immediately.

请放心我们将立即调查此事。

4. oversight：*n.* 疏忽

5. dispatch：*v.* 发送，派遣

Two loads of cloth were dispatched to the factory on 12 December.

12 月 12 日两车毛料被发到工厂。

6. avoid：*v.* 避免

I try to avoid supermarkets on Saturdays - they're always so busy.

我尽量不在周六去超级市场——那时总是人特别多。

We wish to avoid putting you to extra expenses.

我方想避免你方额外的花费。

Sample e-mail 3：Settling a claim for late delivery

From：peter@ keantrading. com
To：carter@ babyclothes. com
Date：Aug. 29，20--
Subject：About the late delivery of S/C No. 65721
Dear Mr. Carter, Your e-mail of August 28，20-- has had our attention. We very much regret that the late delivery[1] has occurred in the execution[2] of your Silicone Baby Bibs[3]. Owing to late arrival of some special raw materials, our production was slightly set back[4]. However，we are glad to inform you that the consignment was shipped this morning，which will arrive at your end on or about October 15. We offer our apologies again for the trouble we brought to you. Best regards， Peter Zhang

NOTES：

1. late delivery：延迟交货

2. execution：*n.* 执行

3. Silicone Baby Bib：婴儿硅胶围兜

4. set back：阻碍

The bad weather set back the building programme by several weeks.

天气恶劣，建筑计划延误了几个星期。

setback：*n.* 挫折，挫败

There has been a slight/temporary setback in our plans.

我们的计划遭到了一点/暂时的挫败。

Useful expressions

Expressing regret over a complaint 对投诉表示歉意
We regret to know that the plastic storage containers arrived damaged on account of improper packaging. 我方遗憾地得知由于包装失误造成塑料整理箱损坏了。 We are sorry to note/hear/learn that 150 pieces of teapots under Order No. 422 arrived in poor condition. 我方遗憾地得知 422 号订单项下的 150 件茶壶到达时损坏了。 We are sorry to learn from your e-mail of October 24, 20-- that you complain about the late delivery of juice extractors you have ordered. 我方从你方 10 月 24 日邮件遗憾地得知你方对订购的榨汁机延迟交货感到不满。 We wish to express our deepest regret over the short delivery of 20 cases of ceramic floor tiles. 我方短交 20 箱陶瓷地砖，对此我方深表歉意。
Explaining causes to the problem 阐述问题产生的原因
On going into the matter thoroughly, we found that a mistake was indeed made in the process of packing through a confusion of quantity. 经彻底调查此事，我方发现该失误是在包装过程中把数量弄混造成的。 This was due to the negligence of our packing staff. 这是我方包装人员的疏忽。 We immediately looked into this matter and studied your Survey Report together with your statement of claims. 我方迅速调查了此事并详细阅读了你方的检验报告和索赔申请书。

It was found that some 40 bags had not been packed in strong paper bags as stipulated in the contract, thus resulting in the breakage during transit.

我方发现大约有 40 袋没有按照合同规定包装在硬纸袋内，导致在运输途中破损。

Taking action to handle complaints 采取措施处理投诉

We are prepared to meet your claim for the 25 tons of shortage weight.

我们准备接受你方就短装 25 吨的索赔。

We are taking immediate action to ship them to you by the first available steamer.

我们将立即采取行动用第一班轮船将货物运往你方。

The replacement of 50 pieces of virtual reality eyeglasses were dispatched to you this morning and will arrive on or about July 3.

替换的 50 副虚拟现实眼镜今天早晨已经运往你方，将在 7 月 3 日左右到达。

We would like to offer you another 20 sets of air humidifiers at 3% discount off the contracted price.

我们想向你方提供另外 20 台空气加湿器，价格在合同价格上给予 3% 的折扣。

Reassuring the buyer of more care for future orders 保证认真处理今后的订单

We assure you that all possible steps will be taken to avoid such mistakes happening again in the future.

我方保证将采取一切可能的措施避免今后再次发生此类事故。

We hope this unfortunate error won't adversely affect the future business between us.

我们希望这次失误不会给我们之间今后的交易带来负面影响。

We wish to assure you that more care will be taken in the execution of your further orders.

我方对此次失误造成的不便深表歉意，保证今后认真执行你方的订单。

We shall do everything we can to ensure that nothing like this will happen again.

我们将尽全力确保此类事情不再发生。

Part 3 Getting prepared for your task

Ⅰ. Pattern drills. Make sentences with the following italicized expressions.

1. *We apologize for* causing you a good deal of inconvenience.

A. 因送抵的货物与发票金额不符，我方深感歉意。

B. 因材料质地与样品相差甚远，我方深感歉意。

C. 因货物短交 20 吨，我方深感歉意。

D. 因部分货物有瑕疵，我方深感歉意。

2. *On going into the matter, we found that* part of your consignment was not packed in

tinned iron boxes.

A. 经调查此事，我方发现发错货物是由于我方包装人员的错误造成的。

B. 经调查此事，我方发现货物的短重是由于包装不当引起的。

C. 经调查此事，我方发现延期发货是由于原材料短缺造成的。

D. 经调查此事，我方发现货物没有按照合同要求包装在硬纸袋内。

3. *We have to lodge a claim* against you *for* the inferior quality of this shipment.

A. 我们不得不对你方发来的第 X－50 号订单货物提出索赔。

B. 我们不得不因为货物在运输途中遭到损坏而向你方提出索赔。

C. 我方不得不对你方这批船货向你提出短重索赔 3000 美元。

D. 我方不得不就这批货物交期延误向快递公司提出索赔 2300 美元。

4. *We assure you that* we are doing all we can to speed delivery.

A. 我们保证会采取有效措施，保护这种商品不被打碎。

B. 我们保证会做好一切必要的安排，按时交货。

C. 我们保证货物包装足够结实，经得起野蛮装卸。

D. 我们保证在今后的交货中不会出现类似的事件。

Ⅱ. Match the sentences related to complaints with the nature of the problems listed in the table.

A. Late/ Non-delivery	D. Inferior quality
B. Shortage	E. Wrong goods delivered
C. Damaged goods	F. Inconformity to sample/contract

1. We are sorry to complain about the inferior quality of the woolen cloth, which seems to be loosely woven and the color is not pure.

2. On examination we found that the consignment did not correspond with the original sample.

3. We regret to have to cancel our order No. 192 owing to your repeated delay in delivery and we have had to purchase the goods elsewhere.

4. The goods we received last week are not up to the standard stipulated in the sales contract. So we have to lodge a claim against you.

5. On opening the cases we found that 80 units of Bluetooth Mini Speakers had been damaged by sea-water, and seem to be complete write-offs.

6. Your failure to deliver the goods within the stipulated time has greatly inconvenienced us. We trust that there will be no repetition of such unpleasant experience in the future.

7. On opening the case we found it contained completely different articles. As we need the goods urgently, we have to ask you to arrange for the dispatch of the replacements at once.

8. Much to our regret, almost every crate was found 5 to 6 lbs short in weight amounting to 200 lbs.

Ⅲ. Read the following e-mail with some problems in it. Then make improvement in terms of spelling, grammar and word choice.

Amy,

We are sorry to learn your letter of the 10th July that 100 pieces of crystal vasesupplied to the above order was damage when they arrived to you. We are regret that it was the problem of improper packing caused. We have already sent replacement to you in this morning and hope they will arrive you next week. To avoid further inconvenience to our customers and extra expense to ourselves, we are taking some measure to ensure the safe arrival of all orders in future. We apologize again for causing you a good deal of inconvenience.

Regards,

Bella Wang

Part 4 Getting your task done

Now please write an e-mail based on your task in Part 1.